FOSTERING

FOSTERING

A MEMOIR OF COURAGE AND HOPE

CARMEN MARÍA NAVARRO

NEW DEGREE PRESS

FOSTERING

A Memoir of Courage and Hope

ISBN   979-8-88504-060-0   *Paperback*

979-8-88504-615-2   *Kindle Ebook*

979-8-88504-165-2   *Ebook*

To Steve, Iago, and Gema.

To my first kids and the kids I love from afar. To Lucy.

To the foster families who choose radical kindness.

To those involved in improving the child welfare system.

And to those who will be inspired to get involved.

CONTENTS

"The true character of society is revealed in how it treats its children."

NELSON MANDELA

~

"I alone cannot change the world, but I can cast a stone across the water to create many ripples."

MOTHER TERESA

PROLOGUE

In 2019, over 670,000 children were touched by the child welfare system. About 250,000 new children entered the system due to abuse or neglect, and after thousands exited, almost 424,000 children still remained in foster care that year. About 122,000 waited to be adopted, and only about 66,000 were adopted that year (AFCARS, 2020).

~

The first time I heard about foster care was when I met my future husband, Steve. It was one of those first dates that got intense pretty quickly. That evening, I shared that I eventually wanted to adopt a kid; he immediately shared his love for his four children and his dream of becoming a foster parent. He asked me, "Why adopt and not foster?"

What is foster? I thought. I knew very little about adoption, but I knew nothing about fostering. Growing up in Peru, families take care of their nieces, nephews, or grandkids. Government-run foster care doesn't exist, and neither does a straightforward translation to the concept. I had no preconceived knowledge.

According to the National Foster Parent Association, "Foster care is the *temporary* placement of children and youth with families outside of their own home due to child abuse or neglect." Adoption is forever.

Both involved helping vulnerable children, which has been a passion of mine since I was sixteen. To graduate from high school, I was required to complete community service hours. So my best friends and I volunteered at a mental institution, supporting children with disabilities. Although it was meant to be for one semester only, we did it for four years until the children were moved to a more suitable group home. Those years had a profound impact on me, and they birthed my deep desire to support youth.

Two years minus one day after we met, Steve and I got married. I became the stepmom of four amazing kids, we had our first biological son, Iago, and we settled as a family of seven. But deep inside, the thought of helping children kept bubbling up. I frequently remembered those volunteering days. I didn't know how or when I would have time to do something that meaningful, but an unsettling feeling we needed to get involved remained. As if being a mom of five children wasn't busy enough. Maybe this was because of them; maybe because we realized not every child is loved or feels safe the way ours did.

When Iago was about three, our last child Gema hadn't been born yet, and I began researching what it meant to adopt and how some people describe it as a beautiful, messy journey. And from what I've seen, it is. It's messy because for an adoption to happen, there is loss—loss for the biological family and for the adoptive child. There is trauma for everyone involved. But it's also beautiful that new forever homes are formed. That from loss comes hope. That some people have the courage to take a leap, proving despite the struggles, love can flourish.

I also learned about the differences between adoption and foster care. Fostering is temporary. Foster parents are meant to provide a safe environment until reunification with the child's biological family can occur. That was compelling and positive. However, it seemed fostering had a negative reputation compared to adoption. In August 2021, I Googled the question, "How is fostering?" The results illustrated the negative bias. It showed what other people were searching for: "Is foster care bad?" "Why do foster parents quit?" and "What is the salary of a foster parent?" I've been asked directly some of those questions; others, I have asked myself as well.

I wonder if the negative reputation of foster care is due to a natural wish for kids to go back to their homes or for them to be adopted. Perhaps it's people's unconscious desire for children to never have to be in this situation.

I wish they were never in that position to begin with. I bet any person with empathy and compassion would believe the same. But the reality is foster care is complex, and it deserves so much more attention and awareness.

The Children's Defense Fund's 2021 report "The State of America's Children" shares "a child is removed every two minutes from their home and placed into foster care," and "on average, a child is abused or neglected every forty-eight seconds in America."

Every two minutes. Every forty-eight seconds.

For every kid adopted in the US, more than five children need foster homes (AFCARS, 2020). Usually, more children enter than exit the foster care system, and their stay could vary from a few months to years. Clearly, there is a constant need for more foster homes. The system needs adults willing to go through months of hurdles to get approved, to take kids who have suffered from immeasurable trauma, families willing to provide a safe place for as long as that child needs it.

Every kid deserves a loving and safe place, from one day to forever, and my wish is every one of those children waiting to be adopted finds their forever home. So why not just adopt?

I confess I go back and forth with this question, and it's a constant struggle. But understanding how large the need for foster homes is, Steve and I decided we wanted to foster so we can impact as many kids as possible. Maybe one day we will end up being that forever home for a child. For now, though, we just want to foster.

And since the plan for more than half of the children is to return to their biological family (AFCARS, 2020), for a significant number of them, the road ahead may still be challenging. If Steve and I, as foster parents, do our jobs right, we will have given the children in our care some new tools for their next phase, and ideally, we would be in their lives as a resource, as their extended family.

Yet my calling has affected my biological kids, and I've come to the difficult realization we need to carefully consider the effects fostering has on our permanent children (bio, step, adoptive), and how critical it is to hear and represent their voices, often forgotten.

A report by the National Conference of State Legislators, estimates that 30 to 50 percent of foster parents quit in the first year, citing lack of support as one of the main causes. In my experience, one aspect in which we lack support is around the permanent children's needs. I wonder if this is true for many foster families and one of their attrition causes.

People have divergent views regarding foster families with permanent kids while fostering. Some people I've interviewed think the foster child benefits from having a dedicated environment, without permanent children in the home, and the foster kid will not feel fully accepted in a house with biological children. Others believe having children in the home will provide a new perspective and show what a healthy relationship with adults could be. It could mean safety and healing in a different way. It could alleviate some of the trauma that comes from being suddenly removed from everything you know and being placed in a home with strangers.

From my perspective, I am hopeful my biological and step kids benefit from the children who come into our home, and we all become better, more empathetic, kinder humans.

But some days I'm full of doubts. Sometimes I feel I'm not good enough to parent my own kids and I question, *How could I be qualified to take care of children who have suffered tremendous trauma?* Other times, I fear my biological children won't feel loved enough or they will resent me for what they had to sacrifice. I fear they could even get hurt in the process.

Truth exists in all points of view. I underestimated how hard this journey is, and I have come to the painful realization the system is not designed to consider the permanent kids in the home, their voices, their needs. I didn't recognize the critical clues and issues my family faced.

My social worker Shonna always asks me, "How are your kids?" We should be asking, "How are *the* kids?" All of them—the foster, the bios, the adoptive, the full foster family ecosystem.

In this book, I not only share the stories of the children who came to our care, but I also share the impact on our whole family, what it means to fall in love with a child and get your heart broken when they leave, what my bio children are teaching me and Steve. I hope it is helpful to others.

I hope by reading this, foster parents will feel and know they're not alone in this journey. I hope the system, which does its best to keep up with the increased needs, also considers the voices of the permanent kids and provides the support required to strengthen the full family.

I ultimately wish any parent, any person who has an interest in the well-being of children feels inspired to learn more and to get involved. Maybe some people will even consider fostering.

We became foster parents hoping we would change lives. I realized almost instantly it's our lives that have changed.

As a foster parent, I quickly discovered it's a much tougher job than I expected. I never thought it was going to be easy, but after a brutal loss—a loss I thought I would never get over—I realized it's much harder than I ever imagined.

It hurts.

And despite knowing the heartbreak, wonderful foster parents keep doing it. Because being a good foster parent means you have to get in deep and love that child unconditionally, fully aware a time may come when you never see them again. It hurts to know every kid who leaves our home will also leave a huge hole in our hearts. It hurts every time and sometimes, it hurts deeply. Yet we do it. As another foster parent in my support group said once, "Our heart breaks so theirs can heal."

The foster care journey is not for the faint of heart. Neither is this book. Fostering is a beautiful, messy, and difficult path. Rewarding and frustrating. This book is about courage and hope. It takes courage to jump into the unknown, to let go of our fears, our self-doubts. It takes courage to do what we do, knowing there will be heartbreak. And it's about hope— hope it will make a difference and even if it hurts, there will be growth and love.

Courage, love, hurt, hope. Repeat.

PART I

BEGINNINGS

CHAPTER 1

THE CALL

It was 2020. Almost a year had gone by since we had gotten approved as foster parents, and suddenly Julianna called.

I was at a work conference call, and without even apologizing, I interrupted my coworker: "I have to get this. My foster care agency is calling!"

I didn't even let them respond and put myself on mute while they signaled it was okay to go, as if their approval was even registering in my mind.

At that precise second, I couldn't care less. It wouldn't have mattered if they would have said, "Hold on one second; the CEO wants to talk with you." All my attention was on the caller ID, fearing it would go to voicemail and we would lose the opportunity to bring a child home.

Because it had already happened. And it happens all the time. If you don't respond right away, you could lose the chance to change your life forever. It's intense. It's a first-come, first-served type of situation, but with people's lives!

This is how it works: The county social worker usually calls or emails their direct contact list and the agencies and shares a small paragraph about the child. It's sad to think a few lines are intended to describe the essence of that kid, basically "sold" in one sentence. The agency in turn will look at their available foster parents and email or call them. If you don't answer, they go on to the next one on the list and the next one until someone responds. The county's goal at that time of crisis is to place that child. And if more than one person responds, they pick the "best candidate." It sounds extremely impersonal because it is. It's like speed dating.

A few months back, after a few failed calls, we got a request for a ten-year-old girl named Valerie, "concurrent" it read, "quiet and good-tempered." "She has an Individual Education Plan (IEP) at school, and is doing well," they added.

I had no idea what "concurrent" meant. I didn't remember that term from our training. But the training had been so overwhelming who knows; maybe we had a full two-hour session about it, and I simply forgot.

"What does 'concurrent' mean again, Julianna?" I asked. All this terminology was so confusing.

"Concurrent to adopt means she is already or may be open for adoption soon, and you need to be willing to adopt," she answered.

I remembered. We had a few hours of training focused on adoption and its process. Concurrent was used when the biological family had lost their parental rights or when it was likely the judge would terminate their rights soon so the child was—or would be—open for adoption. And by "soon," it could be months or years, as the family could appeal and the process could be delayed. It was always unknown.

Foster to adopt? I had not even thought about that possibility. We were in favor of reunification, and Steve and I hadn't talked about adoption since our first date, not even during our foster parent certification process the prior year.

At that second, we were forced to reconsider, and we both felt compelled to say yes. It feels unreal now. But we did—in one phone call that lasted maybe five minutes.

It felt right, despite the potential educational delays and not knowing how she was going to interact with us at home. We didn't want to lose our chance. I don't know why, but at that moment it felt like it could be our only chance.

That night we told our kids a ten-year-old girl was going to come the next day. Her name was Valerie, and she could potentially stay with us a long time, maybe forever, maybe not. We didn't know. The kids asked all the questions you would usually expect: "What's she like?" "What does she look like?" "Where are her parents?" "What grade is she in?" and "Does she know how to play video games?" We couldn't answer anything, but we had instantly fallen in love, the same love we had when I found out I was pregnant. We were excited and nervous. Simultaneously, we were aware of the terrible loss she had suffered if she was available for adoption.

We got ready to pick her up the next day, and it fell through.

Julianna called and shared we had not been selected. I was shocked. We had accepted *all* the unknown conditions, including the possibility to adopt right on the spot.

I couldn't believe it.

The only thing we asked was if we could change her to our school district. We couldn't drive her to a different town at the same time we had to drop off our two kids. Julianna thought it wasn't an issue, but she was going to talk with the county social worker, who was the ultimate decision-maker.

"She is doing so well with her current IEP they don't want her to change schools," Julianna explained.

We understood. Getting an IEP to a point where it works for a child can take a lot of time and effort from all parties. It's another move for her, away from her new support system.

Yet, my heart broke a bit.

I found out later you could ask for help, for someone to drive the kids back and forth to their appointments or their schools. I learned the county approved volunteers who would do this if the foster family has scheduling conflicts. We didn't know this was an option.

Over a month went by after Valerie, and we hadn't received any calls. Although my mind was saying that's a good thing, I was filled with insecurities. *Why didn't they offer a driver if one was available? Are we not suitable to do this?*

They rarely give you an explanation on why we didn't get "the job," so I decided to call Julianna. One of her roles at our agency is to review the incoming requests from the county and determine which of the foster parents could be a good fit. "Julianna, could I please get feedback on why we didn't get Valerie? Is there something we could be doing better?"

There wasn't a particular reason.

With 250,000 new children needing homes every year, across all ages, I struggled to reconcile why there weren't an abundance of calls (AFCARS, 2020).

I realized the more restrictive your requirements are, the more difficult it is to get a placement. We thought we were very open; we signed up for only one girl around Gema's age— who was seven at the time—with no race, sexual orientation, or religious background restriction. It turns out this is very limiting because about two-thirds of the kids in foster care have a sibling who is also in the system, and it is ideal to keep them together (Adopt us Kids, 2021).

If you are not open to sibling groups, to kids with disabilities, to those with sexual abuse history, or if you simply limit the ages or race, it's more challenging. Our foster agency, which operates as our lawyer, tries not to call us if the kids are not close to what we signed up for. It was almost a year since we had been approved as a foster family, and we had gotten very few calls.

While we waited for a stable placement, we decided to open ourselves to do respite. Respite is when a foster child is placed with another approved caregiver for a short period of time, usually less than seventy-two hours, as requested by the child's current foster family (California Department of Social Services, 2021). Respite is a great way to help without a long-term commitment.

A few weeks went by, and I called our main social worker Shonna to ask if there was something "wrong" with us. She explained 2020 was an unusual year because of the pandemic, which was unfortunately detrimental to foster kids in several ways. In some cases, biological parents saw less of their kids as visits had gone virtual, and mental health services and court hearings were delayed. In some states, there was an influx of foster placements, but foster parents were concerned with taking kids exposed to the virus.

Mandated reporters, professionals who interact with children such as teachers or doctors, submit about 70 percent of the reports of neglect or abuse (Child Maltreatment Report, 2019). With the country in a pandemic lockdown, these professionals weren't seeing kids with the same frequency, so the number of reports had diminished.

It was becoming evident the lack of calls didn't imply abuse or neglect wasn't happening. Denise Mann explains in a 2021 US News article "Study: Child Abuse Rose During

COVID Pandemic" school-aged children's physical abuse *tripled* in the pandemic. It makes sense: higher stressors, children locked down at home with no one to see them or speak on behalf of them until it was too late, and a system not prepared to support them during these times.

How devastating!

In the meantime, foster parents like us, available to help, weren't receiving calls.

It's terrible to admit, but when Julianna called this time, my heart started racing and I felt the butterflies. This is the duality of fostering: You get excited when you get a call, and you also feel extremely guilty for those butterflies since you know that child has gone through a terrible ordeal to be in foster care.

"Hi there, I think we finally found the right one. She needs a home for about four months. She has weekly visits with her mom and separate weekly visits with her dad, and the placement is *not* concurrent."

"Not concurrent? Just to be clear, she's not up for adoption?" I was automatically relieved I didn't have to make a life-changing decision at that second.

"Not at this time. Let me read you a bit of her description: 'Five-year-old girl. Loves to sing, dance, and color, likes to help around the house, folds laundry, is very active and energetic. She is a bit defiant at times.' She will be six next month."

That's much more information than we've ever gotten!

More butterflies... my heart was racing even faster. The memory of meeting six-year-old Anya, my stepdaughter, rushed into my mind.

Steve invited me to his house to meet his kids for our second date. Despite our amazing first conversation when we shared our dreams, I had doubts about dating someone with four children. I wasn't prepared for that type of commitment. But somehow Anya changed everything in an instant.

Lacking what my grandma thought was common sense, I drove an hour to his town, found his apartment, and parked almost a block away. Steve was outside playing ball with them, and they seemed to be having a blast.

I hadn't even finished parking, and this little one simply stopped playing, walked a few feet, and looked at me intensely. She was simply adorable, cute as could be. Her brown hair came to just above her shoulders, and she was wearing a striped pink and blue shirt and mismatched aqua leggings. I looked at her, she looked at me, and out of the blue, she gifted me with the most beautiful smile. The sky was cloudy that day, everything was gray and gloomy, but I could swear the sun came out just as she smiled. And those butterflies came rushing out of my heart. At that precise moment, I knew without an ounce of doubt we were going to be in each other's lives forever.

And that's how I felt right then, with Julianna's call, listening about this five-year-old girl needing a home. The same butterflies I felt with Anya. Like it was meant to be.

"One second Julianna. Let me call Steve."

I'm so glad I was on mute because the whole neighborhood heard my scream; I would have burst Julianna's eardrums.

"STEEEEEEEEEEEEEEEVE, STEEEEEEEEEEEEEEVE, come over. It's the agency on the phone!"

Steve came running upstairs, and I'm still not sure if his face was showing excitement because he heard me saying it was the social worker or if he was concerned someone was being murdered by the way I was screaming. His expression was impossible to read.

Either way, Julianna didn't have to wait long

Unmute.

"Julianna, could you please repeat *everything* you said?"

If she was annoyed about repeating herself, I couldn't tell. She had the patience of a saint.

And while Julianna started over, I muted the cell again and without taking a breath, I started rambling over at *warp* speed.

"She's five. We will have her for more or less four months, but who knows." I went on without letting space for any interruption. "She's perfect. She likes to paint, and she sings, and she dances. She will be perfect for Gema; they have so much in common. She is a little bit defiant, but what five-year-old isn't? She will fit right in. If she gets reunified, maybe we can stay in touch. Maybe she won't and we can adopt her. I'm getting ahead of myself. If you don't say yes, I don't think we will get another call. We have to say yes. Ask her when we can pick her up. We need to tell the kids, call the kids! No, no, no. Don't call them. Let's wait. Let's tell the kids when we know for sure. Do you think the kids will be excited?" I paused. I had to breathe.

Damn breathing. Why can't we just go ahead and say everything we need to say without our lungs having to adapt so fast to keep up with our emotions?

I don't think Steve heard much of either one of us, but Julianna asked, "Are you guys open to it? Should I call the county worker and say yes?"

I looked at Steve anxiously. Behind him, there was my bookshelf, and my eyes somehow found the Merriam-Webster dictionary. The golden font had faded, but the red, that velvety red, stared at me. I used to play a game with my grandma when I was little. We used to look up words randomly in that dictionary and their definitions.

Steve looked at me and smiled. I unmuted, trying to sound calm. In unison, we exclaimed, "YES!"

Courage

Noun

cour·age | \ ˈkər-ij , ˈkə-rij \

Definition of *courage*: mental or moral strength to venture, persevere, and withstand danger, fear, or difficulty. (*Merriam-Webster Online Dictionary*)

CHAPTER 2

GETTING STARTED

———

"Did you hear that?" I tapped Steve's arm. "This is voluntary, and we will be *literally* saving a life. It's short-term, so we can still have the house available for the oldest kids and my parents when they come! It's perfect for us!" I slightly increased the pitch with excitement.

It was a night in 2010, and Steve and I were in bed watching TV when a Katie Couric special came on CBS. She was doing a segment on children of the recession, featuring a nonprofit called Safe Families for Children, an organization made of volunteers whose members take care of kids while their parents are unavailable to provide for them. The reasons varied widely: It could be a family was temporarily homeless, a single mother had chemo sessions and was too sick to care for her kids, or a parent was in rehab.

I started to pay attention and pointed at the screen so Steve would listen too. We learned a few things: It was temporary, voluntary, so the motivation wasn't money, and most importantly, it was preventive. We had the opportunity to *prevent* abuse or neglect! How amazing!

"Sounds perfect for us," I exclaimed. "Should I look into it?"

The more you know me, the more you will find out I'm biased to action. So when he nodded distractedly, I took that as a yes quickly before I could regret the decision, or he could regret the implications of what he had just agreed to.

This is what I found: Different from foster care, which is compensated by the state, Safe Families is a nonprofit movement where all families are volunteers. They have supported twenty-five thousand children through the years (Safe Families for Children, 2021). It's important to know once a child enters the foster care system, there is enough evidence abuse or neglect *already* happened. The hope is Safe Families volunteers would provide a safe space for children *before* abuse or neglect took place.

How it works: Parents in crisis voluntarily hand their kids over to this nonprofit so they can be temporarily placed with a volunteer family. The biological parents never lose custody and have the option to take their children back at any time. The duration is considered short-term and varies, ranging from one night to a year. It should be enough time for the parents to overcome their issues. In some cases, Child Protective Services (CPS)—or Department of Children and Family Services (DCFS), the name varies by state—could have been called, but there may not be sufficient evidence to remove the kids from their homes, so Safe Families was presented as an option. Other times, the parent will know of the program and will call asking for help. Meanwhile, the foster care system is not legally involved.

It's an incredible organization because you are certain the families hosting the kids are not doing it for the money, since they're not getting paid. They truly want to help. Meanwhile, the volunteers still go through all the background checks, letters of recommendation, home visits, and training.

We had been living in Pittsburgh, Pennsylvania, for a few years, close to my husband's family. My youngest, Gema, wasn't born yet, and my son, Iago, was in preschool. My bonus kids (my stepchildren) had been coming every summer and holidays, and my parents also visited from Peru once a year. But for a full eight months, the house felt empty; our two extra rooms had unused bunk beds, and it was uncomfortably quiet with just Iago, Steve, and me. The thought of adopting had been sneaking up in the back of my mind for a few years by then. But having "adopted" Steve's kids and having the house full for over three months gave me pause, financially and logistically. I wanted the flexibility to have our extended family visit.

So serendipitous, this TV special. The more I read about it, the more excited I got. It really seemed it would fit our family dynamics.

A few days later, I was disappointed to find out Pittsburgh didn't have a chapter of Safe Families for Children (SFFC). Thankfully, the Chicago SFFC headquarters put me in touch with a foster care and adoption agency in Pittsburgh they had partnered with to start a chapter in our city.

My bias to action and desire to create solutions kicked in, and I immediately volunteered to help with the funding. I became the unofficial development lead for the Pittsburgh chapter, helping raise grants for about $60,000 over the next eight months.

I was consequently invited to the annual fundraising gala for the agency. And that evening, I was fortunate enough to meet Steve Pemberton.

Today, he is a successful executive, family man, author, and advocate; but that evening, he was the keynote speaker sharing his awful experience growing up in foster care. As he described the details of his life, he said something that gave me chills and moved me to the core. He explained when he was really little, he stayed *one* night with a "normal" family, and how that one night gave him a new perspective. As he shared more, the only thing I could think of was how that perspective accompanied him through life and was a positive beacon, despite the years of abuse.

His words, cemented in my heart, would become a continuous reminder of our calling, but it was then my husband and I decided we wanted our home to be that positive reference for children in need. We wanted to give a new perspective, one that could change a kid's path, and possibly lead to a different outcome in life.

It took a few years—Gema to be born, a change of jobs, a move—but we eventually became a Safe Family and ended up hosting five kids during our years in Chicago. The shortest length was a week, the longest, almost ten months. Two years later, we moved to California and eventually fostered a few more children. I know we have given love and safety and provided new perspectives.

Although those are all positive, no one tells you what an emotional roller coaster this is. Even though you know the kind of situation that drives a child to be in your home, no one shares the impact the child has on your heart. Or the uncertainty, the falling in love, the anxiety, the heartbreak, the hope. No one tells you what your family will go through or the impact on your own kids.

Despite how strong this calling is, through the years I have questioned *How do we do good in the world, while protecting the hearts of those who we love the most: our kids?*

It would be something I would discover the hard way.

CHAPTER 3

OUR FIRST CHILD

Andy was our first little one when we started doing Safe Families in Chicago. He was also our first call.

Our social worker at that time asked if we could take a five-year-old boy for just three weeks while his mom recovered from a mental health crisis or if his dad got a more suitable home, whichever happened first.

Anya, who was staying with us for the summer, was old enough to babysit and volunteered to help; in exchange, we offered to pay her as she was saving for college. Gema was a bit over one and Iago was closer to six, so I thought Andy's age was perfect and he would get along well with Iago. They could share a room, and it would be like having a cousin for a few weeks. Steve and I were excited to say yes.

I was naive to think he was going to fit right in and be a temporary playmate. It was a rude awakening.

Paula, Andy's mom, suffered from schizophrenia, her insurance had run out and someone had made a call to the Department of Child and Family Services (DCFS). They issued an investigation, but they didn't find Andy had suffered from abuse or neglect, and he wasn't in immediate danger. However, the situation wasn't good. DCFS convinced

Paula to hand Andy to Safe Families, while she got her insurance sorted out and got back on her medication.

My social worker shared DCFS was concerned about the circumstances: too many people coming in and out of Paula's house, and a few of them with severe mental health issues. *Yep, that doesn't sound good.* I was glad to take part in preventing a child from being harmed.

As it was our first placement, our social worker dropped off Andy that evening and told us to call him if we needed anything; they could take our call 24/7. *I won't need to call; it's going to be fine.* I thought he and Iago would keep each other entertained being so close in age.

Oh boy, was I wrong. I didn't understand the impact childhood trauma has on the brain's development.

Andy behaved in line with a two-year-old, much closer to Gema's age.

The article "The Biological Effects of Childhood Trauma," by Dr. Michael D. De Bellis and Abigail Zisk, shares children's brain functions are impacted significantly if they have witnessed violence or have been exposed to any event that will cause them trauma. Areas of the hypothalamus are affected, which will meaningfully delay the child's development, to the point a five-year-old could behave like a two-or-three-year-old.

At first glance, Andy seemed fine. He was soft-mannered and agreeable. He was easy to love. He would hold my hand with infinite trust. He had beautiful dark blue eyes and brown hair with an almond-shaped face and a smile never fully formed. I started to realize I had never heard him laugh. It seemed he looked past us into emptiness. He barely spoke, and when he did, it was merely a whisper.

He needed help with almost everything but didn't fight you when you offered. He let me shower him, change him, brush his teeth, and put him to bed.

And what an appetite! That seemed to be the only aspect in which he operated independently—except he didn't know how to use a fork or a spoon. He would grab a handful of mac and cheese with his hands and swallow voraciously. Did he even chew? I don't think I ever saw him chew! And he wasn't picky either, so we expanded our menu repertoire to chicken with broccoli or chili and he would eat it all, which surprised me the most!

Our social worker dropped him off with a garbage bag with just a few things in it: some old underwear, a few mismatching socks, a couple of shorts, and maybe two stained t-shirts. No pajamas, no stuffies, no toys. I immediately noticed his sandals were too small for his feet because his toes were fully sticking out and were dirty. Iago and Gema were very welcoming; they both hugged him and wanted to play with him right away. He was okay with the attention and wasn't scared. It was clear he was used to many people around him. He went with them to our family room and sat on the floor to play, looking at them but not interacting much.

That first night I grabbed some pajamas from one of the drawers, and without much thought, I told Iago Andy hadn't brought any pajamas and he was borrowing them for the night. They were about the same size, and I figured they could share. Iago simply said, "Okay." I assumed he was preoccupied with the new playmate, rather than what was going on in his dresser. I made sure I didn't grab any of his superhero ones; just the green dinosaur ones he didn't care for. The next day, while the kids and Steve were all getting breakfast, I looked further in the closet for anything that could fit Andy. Iago had two pairs of similar tennis shoes, so I took one and put it aside for when I got Andy dressed.

Later that morning, Iago burst into my room. "*Mami!* Why is Andy wearing my shoes and my clothes?"

I was ready for this moment! "Because he doesn't have a lot, *amor*. He came with just a few things, and I'm doing his laundry. We said we were going to share when new kids came."

"You're not doing laundry of his shoes. I saw his shoes in the closet," he quickly replied.

"Yes, *amor*, his sandals don't really fit him anymore, and you have two pairs of tennis shoes. I thought you could give him one. Don't you want to share?" I answered confidently.

"Yes, *Mami*, I can give him my shoes, I can give him my clothes. But next time, please ask me." He turned around and left the room.

Oh my goodness!

My five-year-old had just given me a master lesson on boundaries and respect! Why hadn't I considered his feelings, his thoughts? These were his things! I hadn't stopped to think how this was going to impact Iago or Gema. From sharing a room, to sharing clothes, to sharing their parents' time.

Our training was insufficient on this matter, and our biological children were an afterthought. I didn't ask; I thought kids are resilient. It didn't occur to me this would affect them as much as it affects me. Now I know the full family needs to be considered, *especially* our kids, who, despite not signing up for this job, are the most impacted by it.

~

"*Mami*, why do you say 'I love you' to Andy too? Do you love him?" asked Iago one night after I put Andy to bed.

"Because he probably misses his mommy and I want to make sure he knows we love him," I replied.

"But do YOU love him? Or are you just saying that? Do you love him like me?"

What a hard question! Of course I didn't love him as much, especially after only a few weeks, but every kid deserves to be loved, so I decided to just say it until I felt it. I didn't know if I would ever love my temporary kids the same way as I love my own, but did it matter?

"Iago worries about Iago." I quickly added, "I love you, *amor*, more and more and more every day." This was a polite way to say, "mind your own business." I hope that settled it.

~

"*Mami*, there is poop all over the wall. It smells really bad," Iago shouted a couple of days later.

"What?" I asked incredulously.

"There is poop on the wall in the bathroom, on the way to my bedroom, in my bedroom. It wasn't me. I don't think it was Gema. I think it was Andy," he replied.

It had been Andy... I'm not sure if he was trying to call attention to himself, rebelling, or showing his pain, but there was poop smeared everywhere. That night, Iago didn't want to sleep in his room. He slept with us. The next day we told our social worker.

~

"*Mami*, Andy is yelling at the walls," Iago shared another day.

I didn't doubt it this time... With Paula being schizophrenic, maybe he was not yet diagnosed. Can you diagnose something like that in kids? Are they too small? We texted our social worker.

~

"*Mami*, I know Andy is five, but why is his brain like a baby's brain?" Iago asked toward the end of the three weeks.

Oh, sweet boy. Sweet, perceptive child. *Because of child trauma, mi amor,* I wanted to say. I can't recall what I answered. I think I mumbled some kids are born like that, and we are all different. Are they though? Some are... but others? The way Andy behaved left me thinking he had been much more exposed to neglect or trauma than we originally thought, and it was much harder on my children than what we had considered.

Andy left after the three weeks. A month later, Safe Families called and told us his return home hadn't worked out and his parents still needed help, and they asked if we could take him back for a few months. Iago overheard the conversation and pulled my shirt whispering, "No, *Mami*, please no. I like him a bit, but not so much. Please say no."

Andy didn't come back. It was hard to say no, but I had promised myself to consider my children's input moving forward.

CHAPTER 4

WRECK-IT RALPH

"How is Danny doing?" my mom asked when she came during her annual visit from Peru. She had gotten to know him in the month my parents stayed with us the prior year in Chicago. I hadn't seen Danny in over a year since we moved to California.

"Do you miss him?" Straight to the point! She always asks, always concerned if I'm doing well, if I'm hurting.

A rush of emotions filled my heart the minute I heard his name. My Danny! My beautiful boy... of course I missed him. He was such a large part of our family and is still a large piece of my heart. How could I not?

"Sometimes... But I don't miss him that much, Ma," I lied.

I had to lie to myself as well. I had to put all those feelings in my imaginary wooden jewelry box and throw the keys far, far away, so I could keep going. The same way I do today with things that cause me anxiety or sadness.

~

Danny came to our home early one summer, when we were still in Chicago, almost a full year after Andy had left. Iago was almost seven, Gema two. He was our first long-term placement; he stayed with us for about ten months. And he was the first placement who broke my heart.

One evening I answered a call from our social worker at Safe Families. It was about a six-year-old boy who needed a home for a few months. No more details were given except he could fit very well with our family. I had learned, through our experience with Andy and the other children we hosted, there was no such thing as a "fits well with the family" in circumstances of children removed from their homes. They always carry some type of trauma that makes it challenging.

Danny would later prove me wrong. He *was* the perfect fit.

I shared it with Iago and Steve, and we decided to say yes. Later that evening, a county social worker named Sonya called me and asked if we could meet the next day at the police station near my house. Since it was the following day, I didn't think it was an emergency, but it bothered me the exchange had to be done in a police station. *That's no place for a child.*

I took the day off and arrived at the station at 10 a.m. sharp. I didn't want to be late. Outside of the front door, there was a small patio with red brick walls. Standing next to a metal bench, a younger couple and a scared-looking little boy were talking to a woman with short gray hair, dressed in khaki pants and a white polo. Her voice was deep and coarse, but her tone was soft and kind. I caught the end of her sentence: "...a few months maybe. We will see."

"Are you Sonya?" I asked while approaching, curiously glancing at the child. He looked down.

"Thank you for coming. This is Danny, and these are his aunt and uncle." Her tone changed halfway through that introduction right at the word *aunt...* unapproving, almost like condemning them.

They all shook my hand except for Danny, who grabbed his backpack tightly and stood still. I could only see the top of his head, his light brown hair.

"Let me get the paperwork for you to sign. It's in my car," Sonya said.

The uncle put his arm on Danny's shoulder, and his aunt lowered herself into a squat and muttered something I couldn't hear. He didn't look at them.

"Are you family then?" I asked, puzzled. *Why would they take this kid away from an aunt or an uncle? Under what circumstance would I turn my back on my nephew or my niece?* I would keep them without a doubt.

His aunt stood up and embarrassingly said, "Yes, we are. His dad is my cousin." *Would I turn away my cousin's kids? What if it was a distant cousin and I didn't have the means?* Doubt hit me. *I shouldn't judge if I can't answer that question myself.*

I squatted to Danny's level and said, "Hi, I'm Carmen-Maria. You can also call me CM, whatever you prefer."

It was all handled outside the police station and the exchange of paperwork didn't last long. Sonya said she was going to give me a call later to check in before the court hearing in a few weeks. "Later" was undefined. I was confused. This was a voluntary situation. DCFS was not officially involved, but she gave me her card in case I needed anything. If the county wasn't involved, why was Sonya handling everything and not Safe Families? I didn't feel it was appropriate to ask her with the child standing next to us. I wanted to take him out of that place as soon as possible.

~

Danny had an instant connection with both Gema and Iago. That afternoon they played outside with the hose. It wasn't exactly warm, and I could see their hands and lips turning blue, but they didn't care. I didn't want to say anything; I was trying to balance the apparent joy of that moment with the insecurities about my parenting. *Would they get pneumonia?* I pushed away that thought. *They're bonding.* I kept that one.

Based on that afternoon, I didn't expect the first night to be as rough. Danny was on a call with his dad for hours and wouldn't stop crying. His dad had given him a phone, and since this was a voluntary relinquishment of his kid to strangers, I was unsure of which rules applied.

In foster care, the child's property must be respected, such as a phone. The child also has the right to confidential calls unless otherwise specified by the court (Youth Law Center, 2018). As a foster parent, I can determine what's age-appropriate usage and restrict the schedule of the phone. But Danny wasn't technically in foster care, and with his dad voluntarily handing his son over to Safe Families, it was undefined.

He talked with his dad every night with no time limit or supervision. And from the child and the parent's perspectives, that's how it should be. But from my perspective, it was difficult. Iago and Danny shared a room, and Iago listened to Danny cry *every* night for hours while on the phone with his dad. Iago also questioned why Danny had a tablet and a phone and he didn't.

Although things improved with time, it was very tough before it got better. Danny was, generally speaking, easy. As easy as any kid who has suffered trauma could possibly be.

Every night, he would call his dad and synchronize to watch a movie together: *Wreck-It Ralph*. The same Disney movie, *every* night. They would set up the starting time of the movie at minute 3:03 exactly.

Danny would say, "Go," and press play, and his dad would attempt to press play at the same exact second. But if Wreck-It Ralph's voice was a millisecond off, if the exact word was not in *exact* synchrony with the word on the other side of the phone, it was chaos!

Danny would yell, "Noooo, we need to do it again!" and the agony would start over. He would pause, rewind, stop, cry, start over, pause, rewind, cry. Steve would take Iago to our room so he could sleep in our bed while I stayed on the floor, next to Danny's bed through all of it. Start, pause, rewind, scream, one melatonin, start, pause, rewind, another melatonin, cries on both sides of the phone. Desperation... "I'm trying, buddy, I'm trying," his dad would say. And after a couple of hours or so, his dad would say, "I have to hang up, buddy," and eventually they would hang up.

I would be there, just waiting for this awful night to be over. Every night. There was nothing I could do. Nothing. And it broke my heart, just as my mom predicted, but I'm sure his dad's heart was decimated every time Wreck-it Ralph said, "Hi."

CHAPTER 5

CO-PARENTING

"Ongoing investigation."

The second I heard those words from the county's social worker, I became concerned. It turned out Danny had been removed from his parents' house because his oldest brother, whom he idolized, had died, and the county was investigating the cause of death.

In our training they teach us not to judge and to be supportive of the biological family, and I was trying so hard to be supportive and nonjudgmental, but it was freaking hard. I didn't know his parents, and I was concerned we had to see them regularly when we took Danny to his visits. I was worried about our safety, especially since Danny shared identifiable information, like what type of neighborhood we lived in, what school he was going to, what he saw when he walked out of our house.

My mind kept going back and forth from one extreme to another, from *Could his dad be a killer?* to *It must be devastating for him and his family.*

I reflected on the situation. I couldn't imagine what it would be like to have one of my babies die and the other one, taken away. Or what it would be like for one of my kids to suddenly lose a sibling and, immediately after, lose every-thing they know and move into a house with strangers. It's heartbreaking. That's how it is for so many kids in the system.

It's not their fault they lose everything. It's never their fault.

~

Over the next few months, my level of comfort improved, and so did our nightly routine. I'm not sure if it was because Danny and his dad got better at synchronizing the start of the movie or because time calmed things down. Regardless of the reason, Iago went back to sleeping in his room, and I heard more laughs late at night than what I would usually allow. I didn't complain or tell them to go back to bed. I was just happy to hear a sense of normalcy.

Mornings and nights became fun. All three kids would show up on my bed for morning or bedtime hugs and kisses. Danny was becoming one of us.

We even got his parents to give us permission to take him on a vacation trip; and despite our doubts, we made an effort to invite them to see Danny every chance we could. At first, it started with a few hours in a park nearby, but once I felt better about our overall safety, they started to come to our home.

After about four months, I got a call from Danny's social worker, Sonya, asking if we could take him as our foster son. He was formally entering the system.

"What happened? How? We're not certified as a foster family. We are just a Safe Family. I don't think we meet the minimum training requirements. We don't have the paper-work. I would love to. *We* would love to, but I don't think we can, at least not in time. Or can we?" I rambled.

"Yes, if you're willing to keep him, we can give you *kinship care* status and you will have time to get certified. The process is easier than getting a regular foster parent license."

"I'm sorry. What is kinship?" I muttered.

Sonya quickly answered, "Kinship is foster care for family members. We were in court, and Danny is formally entering the foster care system. This is going to take a while. His parents said you're his godmother. It's a loophole in the law. As godmother, you're considered a family member, and you can keep Danny if you agree."

Kinship care had been increasing in Illinois over time, and later that year, in June 2015, Illinois DCFS passed the new Fictive Kin Law, where they expanded the definition of family to include people unrelated by birth or marriage, who had a relationship with the child or the child's family. By 2018, the percentage of kids in foster care living with non-relatives was 44 percent, down from 53 percent in 2012 (Shelton, 2018).

"Absolutely we can keep him," I replied trying to control my voice suddenly shaking, feeling immense sadness for Danny's parents. Conversely, I was thankful kinship was an alternative.

The loophole became the law. The loophole brought us together and made us a family.

~

As time went on, Iago and Danny acted more and more like typical brothers, playing, fighting, laughing, competing, very much competing! Both boys were signed up in hockey, soccer, baseball, and each was trying to demonstrate who was better—who threw the ball further, who hit the puck more accurately, who skated without falling, who was more helpful around the house, who made us laugh louder... who was more of our son.

As competitive as they were with each other, they were both so patient and gentle with Gema. Danny treated her like a doll, and Gema called them both "ma boys." They were both her brothers, with no distinction, and Danny had become our child.

Later, it was the adults who, little by little, became friends, evolving our relationship from strangers to co-parents, building a different kind of friendship. A friendship born out of grief, empathy, and love.

We celebrated birthdays, first Danny's, then Gema's. We even had a few awkward dinners to celebrate the adults' anniversaries and Christmas. All of us did a wonderful job maintaining as much stability as possible, and as time went by, *Wreck-it Ralph* stopped being the main character of our nights.

But despite all this love and empathy, I hid a secret.

CHAPTER 6

HOPE

"Danny's next court hearing is coming up, and I am recommending termination of parental rights. We may even press charges. If that goes through, would you be willing to adopt him?" Sonya asked. He had been with us for over eight months by then.

What? How is this happening? Termination of parental rights?

I didn't understand. I had gotten to know Danny's parents, and they were both loving, kind, and respectful. It was evident they loved their son. They couldn't talk about the investigation surrounding their oldest son's death and I didn't pry, but in my gut, I felt they had nothing to do with it. The way they treated us, how they treated my kids... I couldn't see a reason why they would take Danny permanently away from them. So when the county social worker shared that news, I was in shock.

"Yes, but why?" I asked, struggling to understand, with many mixed feelings: betrayal, sadness, and a bit of relief I wasn't going to lose a boy whom I had grown to love, a boy whom my kids saw as their sibling.

"I can't say anything else, but I want to know if he has a home with you?" she insisted.

Of course he has a home with us. I didn't want to sound eager to keep him. "Whatever you need, we want what's best for him," I replied.

~

"How do we tell the kids?" I asked Steve the same night.

"Well, we'll just have to explain to them he is part of our family, a brother, and he will be staying. We can tell them little by little. We can start planting the seed," he said.

I wondered if Danny's dad suspected anything. We had become somewhat friends. I pushed away that thought.

The next day we started introducing new nomenclature at home: "our kids" and "your brothers" versus "the boys." Later, we started talking to the boys about the future, when they grew up. One day Iago asked if Danny was staying forever, and I said, "Maybe yes."

Over the next month, I avoided Danny's usual questions about when he was going back home, about his mom, his dad, or his friends from his other house. So many unanswered questions. Regardless of how I answered, it would break someone's heart, probably more than one.

In the meantime, we continued the weekly visits at our home. There was no mention of courts or deadlines. But we all knew something loomed. We were just avoiding the inevitable while doing our best to co-parent. I wondered if his dad thought "the inevitable" would have a different outcome than what I expected to happen. Guilt consumed me. It was like having a double life.

A month later, the court hearing arrived. It was scheduled for 1 p.m. We would hear from the social worker at around 3 p.m.

At about 2:30 p.m., my cell phone rang, and it was Danny's dad: "It's over! They've cleared us from all wrongdoing. They've declared our son's death an accident! We got Danny back! We're on our way to pick him up! Thank you for everything!"

The world stopped.

Thank you for everything... He's my son too. This is not an invite for dinner where you say thanks for everything.

I couldn't hear anything else; I don't recall what I said back. I just hope I was graceful, but I can't even say if I was. The call was interrupted by a text from Sonya saying he was returning to his parents, and she would pick up the paperwork "at a later date."

A little bit later, Danny's parents arrived, and they packed all his things in fewer than thirty minutes. We took a picture outside the house to celebrate his return home. Danny wouldn't look at me when he gave us all rushed hugs. They got in their car and left.

After almost ten months of love.

Just like that, by 3:30 p.m., within an hour, he was gone. He was simply gone.

I walked up the stairs trying to keep it together, holding back my tears. I was shaking, and I didn't want Iago and Gema to see me. My heart was heavy, and I felt physical pressure on my chest, making it hard to breathe. I went to the boys' bedroom to clean up. *Iago's bedroom*, I reminded myself.

The room looked like an earthquake had hit. The closet door was open, empty hangers on the left side, some had fallen to the floor, one broken. Most likely because whatever piece of clothing that was there had been ripped off in a hurry. One of the drawers of the black dresser was opened. A pair of socks neatly packed in the shape of a ball had fallen off to the floor. Danny's pajamas were still under his pillow. Most of his toys were gone.

I heard Steve telling Iago not to worry, we would see Danny that upcoming weekend in their baseball game and the rest of the baseball season. His dad had confirmed Danny was going to remain on the team, where Steve was the coach. That night I asked both Iago and Gema if they wanted to sleep with us, and they said yes. We were all grieving. If I'm being honest, they were doing me a favor. I wanted to feel their warm squirmy bodies next to me, so I wouldn't spend all night crying. I had to keep busy and focused on my own kids. *Danny is mine too. No, he's not. I was just his mom for a season. He was just borrowed. Where is my imaginary jewelry box? Why can't I find it and hide this sorrow?*

~

The next months were extremely tough for me. I missed our daily family routines, the laughs, the noise. The house was quieter; the dinner table felt empty with just the four of us. Steve and the kids settled into the new reality rather quickly. During baseball practices or games, the only opportunity to see Danny, he was loving toward Gema; respectful with Steve, as his coach; a bit standoffish with Iago, which I'm sure was hurtful; but with me... I was plainly ignored.

While he had been at our home, I had taken Danny to see a child grief counselor. I called her to cancel his future appointments and shared, "He's ignoring me. Is it normal?"

"Yes, it is. It's his defense mechanism. He most likely feels he's betraying his mom if he shows you love. It may get better in the future."

It may get better in the future? It's normal? I'm dying. I can't get out of bed in the mornings.

"You have just suffered a loss, and you need to grieve. It takes time. Take the time," she added kindly.

I kept asking Steve, "Don't you miss him?"

His usual response was, "We did our job." He never really said if he missed Danny or not. "Our job" doesn't even begin to describe the overwhelming feeling of loss.

I know I can't compare my loss with that of parents who have lost a child. I can't compare my loss to Danny's parents losing their oldest son. I can't. I know Danny's alive, where he belongs—with his parents. He's safe and loved. His grades are good, he does all the sports in the world, and from what I see on Facebook, he's good at all of them. I'm not saying his life is perfect or will ever be because of this traumatic experience, and we know trauma causes long-term consequences. I think he will be forever marked by the loss of his brother and the temporary loss of his home. His childhood was disrupted, and his home will *never* be the same.

But I did lose him as well. I lost a child. He is their son, my son, our son.

It's been years since he left our home. *Years.* And I am so happy for him. Despite the sense of loss, I was happy back then, and I'm happy now. He's back where he was supposed to be, with his biological parents, who love him and went through a terrible ordeal to get him back.

I know it's how it should be, but it's not easy. I still hated to hear in our latest foster parent training, "Remember, the end goal is reunification." *I know! I've lived it!* I also hate it when people tell me we accomplished what we needed to accomplish—when they say, "You did well. You kept him safe and now he's back home," or when someone asks, "Isn't that the goal, though?"

I know that. But can't it still hurt? Can't I mourn the loss of a child, the loss of a possibility of what could have been? A child whom I loved, whom I still love? I have the right to grieve.

The job, as Steve calls it, is hard.

So when my mom asked when she came to visit California over a year later, "Do you miss him?" I lied.

Because even though it tore me apart, we won't stop doing this. We don't want to because we believe we're making a difference. Danny went back home to his parents. It was the best possible outcome. He is safe and loved. And while he was with us, he was safe and loved as well. Despite how much it hurts, we do this because, whether if it's for one night or for as long as Danny was with us, there is hope of a better outcome.

Hope
verb
\ ˈhōp \
hoped; hoping
Essential meaning of *hope*: to want something to happen or be true and think that it could happen or be true.
(*Merriam-Webster Online Dictionary*)

PART II

LUCY

CHAPTER 7

LOADING ONLY

———

I picked up Lucy at the Family Crisis Center on a Thursday afternoon in September 2020.

I was nervous.

It had been years since Danny had been reunified with his parents, and a lot had happened. We moved from Chicago to California; I needed time to heal and to get settled in our new home. Our town didn't have Safe Families, so we were unsure of our path forward. In the meantime, I volunteered on a board of a nonprofit supporting homeless youth and the issues surrounding children who age out of foster care without a family.

After four years of resting, exploring, and finding the right agency, we got certified as foster parents. Getting Lucy's call took another year.

Julianna, one of our social workers, had called two days before, and I had to rearrange my work schedule to pick Lucy up. Although Steve was available, I wanted to get her myself. As I've learned, over 18 percent of the children have been physically abused, 9 percent sexually abused, and about 30 percent have domestic abuse in their background (Children's Bureau, 2020). So those first interactions are critical. In my experience, kids react differently to foster parents' genders. Some feel more at ease with me, especially if one of our biological kids is there, so Steve and I arranged for him to bring Gema to the Family Crisis Center after school and homework.

As I was driving to the Center, I became concerned about running into Lucy's biological parents. I called Shonna, our main social worker, and she shared there were two entrances to the building: one for bio parents, the other for the kids and caregivers. I sighed with relief but couldn't shake off the nerves.

I arrived. The parking lot was full. *So many kids*, I thought. I looked around and found a parking space a few yards from the entrance with a sign that said, "Loading Only." *Would this little one think I consider her "cargo"?* And I thought, *She's just five. Most likely she doesn't know how to read.*

But that obsessive, irrational thought kept coming back and took a life of its own.

How about the person dropping her off? Would she think I think she's "cargo"? Would she be concerned I'm not the right foster mom? Why do I think she's a "she"? It could be a "he" or a "they"? Guys and queer people can also be foster parents. Why am I discriminating? Do I usually discriminate like this?

It was getting late, so I got out of the car. A large fenced empty playground was to my right. I walked toward the entrance where people were coming in and out: children holding hands with adults, teenagers walking at some distance from their foster parents, county workers wearing badges. Since it was the peak of the pandemic, everyone wore masks, making them all expressionless.

As I entered the building, I felt uneasy. It was no better than the police station where I picked up Danny back in Chicago years earlier. This was the first time I had been to any Family Crisis Center, and I had this preconceived notion it would be full of color, light, and laughter. I wonder why I thought it would be that way. Maybe my unconscious was optimistic and hoped anything related to kids was equivalent to joy. Unfortunately, as I've learned through the years, foster care is the opposite.

It was dark. I don't know if they were saving on electricity, the light bulbs were not bright enough, or it was too sunny outside, but it took a few seconds for my eyes to adjust. Although the walls were colorful—red, orange, green, and beige—they were stained, and the gray carpet was worn out. It smelled musty, dirty. I heard a kid screaming. I frowned.

At a security booth in front of me, a woman was on the phone purposefully avoiding looking at people. I tried to make eye contact, but she looked away. There was a single metal chair to the left and a black foldable table to the right where some adults and children were in line to check in. They all knew what to do except for me. Like robots on autopilot. *Was I going to be like that in a few months?* Another security guard measured a young kid's temperature with a yellow thermometer that looked like a large drill, while a woman next to him signed the visitor log with a light blue pen with a chewed top. *I should have brought my own pen.*

I was next. I looked around for hand sanitizer and found some next to the booth. I needed to stay six feet apart, but there wasn't enough space. Despite the high ceilings, the strange-smelling air wasn't circulating.

At that moment, I had to remind myself *I* had offered to pick her up.

When I walked toward the security guard, he asked me to sign in and took my temperature with the "drill" while I answered the routine COVID questions. I told him I was coming to pick up a little one and gave the social worker's name.

He asked me to take a seat, pointing at the metal chair. I looked around to see if anyone else needed it, but the people in line ahead of me were already gone. As I waited, I wondered where the butterflies were that I had felt the days before, now replaced by so many unsettling thoughts and questions I had forgotten to ask Shonna.

How's it going to be for Gema and Iago? Will they all get along? Are we her second house? Why did she leave her prior house? What race is she? If she's a Black little one, how would I know how to do her hair? I need to get educated and watch some online videos or find a place that could do her hair. Will she have clothes, or do I need to stop at Target tonight? I hope she doesn't leave poop all over the wall like Andy. What if she's thirsty? I should have brought a bottle of water. Or hungry? Will she eat McDonald's? All kids like McDonald's. But what if she doesn't? What if the only thing she eats is McDonald's? What will I feed her? I can't force her to eat broccoli. That's illegal. I can't force her to eat anything! I will have to complement McDonald's with some vitamins. I think I can give her vitamins, can't I? Oh no, the training said I need to get a doctor's prescription for over-the-counter medications. Are vitamins over the counter? How about a Band-Aid? I forgot to ask if she takes any medication. If she takes medication, I hope it's not refrigerated; I don't have the medicine lockbox for the fridge. I'm glad Shonna didn't check that in our last home inspection. I may need to take her to the doctor to get that vitamin prescription. I need to remember to ask all of this. I need to write this down. Oh no! I also forgot a notebook. I should've brought a notebook. Maybe I have a piece of paper in the car I can write on, and a pen with no chewed top. Did I have time to go back to the car and check? Did I put the booster seat in the back? What was the California law for car seats? OH MY GOODNESS, I am forgetting all about being a parent. I feel so inadequate. I need to call Steve.

"Are you Carmen?" A good-looking, young brunette with beautiful long hair and a white binder interrupted my thoughts. "I'm Emily, Lucy's social worker."

How young is this woman? Does she have a lot of experience dealing with kids? Here comes my bias again! Don't judge; she's probably perfectly capable, and you're already judging her.

"Oh, nice to meet you. I'm CarmenMaria. I go by both names." *Should I have corrected her on my name in my first meeting? She's going to feel awkward, and the relationship won't start well. I should have waited.*

Not showing one ounce of awkwardness, Emily asked, "Sorry about that, CarmenMaria. Let's go outside and review the paperwork. Lucy should be here any minute. Where did you park?"

Oh, no! If she sees me parked in the "Loading Only" section, she will think I think these kids are things to load and unload. Mere objects. I should say something. Maybe I should say, "I really do not feel she's cargo. She's a human being, and I hope you know I'm a very qualified foster parent. Although this is our first full-time placement in this state, I have raised at least seven kids. I'm very qualified." Why did I park there? I should have parked in the regular human section. Not in the unloading and loading section. Fuck!

We headed outside, and I quickly scouted the place. I thought I had seen a bench as I passed the playground. Yes, there it was, right next to the "Loading Only" parking spots.

We sat down, and I thought she was going to hand me the white binder with all Lucy's information, but I was mistaken.

She pulled out *one single* piece of paper with the addresses and times of all the appointments, which she proceeded to read out loud.

- Mondays at 2 p.m.: therapy center (which I later found out was for kids who had been sexually abused). Phone number and therapist name.
- Monday at 3 p.m.: visit with the dad every other week in person at the therapy center; at 5 p.m. every other week via Zoom. Phone number of the Crisis Center.
- Fridays at 3 p.m.: visit with the mom every other week in person at the Crisis Center; at 5 p.m. every other week via Zoom. Phone number of the Crisis Center.
- The phone number of clinician services from the prior county, whom I needed to call and ask if they could come to this county to give her services.

Emily mentioned she would visit our house to check on Lucy the following week, and she would *try* to visit every month, but she couldn't promise because of the pandemic.

I needed to set up dentist and doctor appointments right after her birthday, which was in October, and I should email her once I had them all booked.

How am I going to remember all of this? I should have stolen that nasty pen with the chewed top.

"You work with an agency, don't you? Your social worker will send the insurance card. Any questions?" Before I could answer, she said, "Oh, there she is... Ah, forgot to mention, sometimes you will have to be a little bit stern with her. That seems to have worked in prior houses."

She's here! Butterflies. Finally.

What did she just say? What does she mean by prior houses, plural? How many houses are we talking about? These kids should be stable in one house and not be moved around.

I read in the article "What Impacts Placement Stability?" from *Casey Family Programs* only around 40 percent of children stay in fewer than two houses— "one too many," they say. And the longer they are in the system, the more houses (placements) they have, the more trauma they experience, the worse their future looks.

When I heard Emily say "houses," I thought of another foster parent who shared he fostered a set of siblings who were eight and five, and his had been their *thirteenth* home! Later he fostered another group of siblings, seven and two, and his home was their *eleventh* placement. Both times, the county didn't share this information with him before placing the children.

Emily had definitely said "houses." *How long has Lucy been in the system? She is just five.*

While I was asking myself all these questions, an energetic little girl came running out of a silver SUV that had just parked in the "Loading Only" space, next to my car. She had bright blue eyes and long blond hair tied in a ponytail with a pink bow. She wore pink shorts, a pink t-shirt with a colorful unicorn, and light blue worn-out tennis shoes.

Without saying hi, she went past Emily directly to the playground, swung the gate open, and jumped on a swing. She clearly knew her way around. An older woman with gray hair and cat-eye sunglasses in a casual floral white-and-gray dress got out of the car and asked the little girl to slow down. She didn't; she kept running.

Ha! She parked in the same section. Is she the current foster mother? Is she getting rid of Lucy, like a load, a thing? Why would I think that? Why would I automatically think she's getting rid of her? Is someone getting rid of her? How many houses had Lucy been at? This girl looks alright—clearly energetic but alright. Why would anyone get rid of a precious little one and move them from house to house like an object? Why am I judging? I need to make sure I get her cell number so I can get more information than what I just got from Emily.

Emily tried to stop Lucy as she ran by her, quickly realizing it was going to be an impossible task, so she turned back to me and said, "Let's just leave her there while we transfer her things to your car."

The lady in gray waved and said, "Hi, I'm Jackie. I'm Lucy's transport. I have her things in the back. She has a lot. Where is your car?"

Right here in the "Loading Only" section next to yours.

We most likely parked there because it's close to the door. I had gotten so worked up about it. As if my parental skills were defined completely and exclusively by my parking selection. I guess we're quick to say how things *should* be—quick to judge, including judging ourselves too harshly. But in fostering, I feel at some point we all judge each other—biological parents, foster parents, social workers, foster kids, outsiders. I would later learn judging ourselves or others is as meaningless as the selection of that parking spot.

Judgment
noun
judg·ment | \ ˈjəj-mənt \
Definition of *judgment*
   1. a. the process of forming an opinion or evaluation by discerning and comparing
      b. an opinion or estimate so formed
   (*Merriam-Webster Online Dictionary*)

CHAPTER 8

FIFTEEN-MINUTE EXCHANGE

DAY ONE

"Hi, I'm CarmenMaria. I parked next to you," I responded to Jackie as she approached and shook my hand.

"Nice to meet you, CarmenMaria," she replied.

I was about to offer her a spot on the bench so we could chat for a bit, but she was all business. She turned around, clicked her car key, and opened the back of her SUV. Lucy had a lot of things. *We picked the right parking spots after all.* I smiled.

Emily walked toward the playground while Jackie and I spent about ten minutes getting Lucy's worldly possessions into the back of my SUV. Jackie had been kind enough to pack her things in tubs and in cardboard boxes.

"These are my tubs. At least they're not garbage bags," she mentioned. I didn't understand the comment then. I immediately thought *Why would she say something like that? Does she want the tubs back? Oh...* I realized if Jackie was the "transport," she must have picked Lucy up with her things in garbage bags, like little Andy, who came to our home in Chicago with his few things in a garbage bag. My heart sunk a bit.

This is one of the hard realities of foster care. When children are removed from their homes with very little notice, they generally grab whatever they can and put them in pillowcases or garbage bags. It probably happens too often because nonprofits such as Comfort Cases or the She Ready Foundation provide suitcases and backpacks as a way to bring dignity to foster children. In an interview between David Letterman, television host, and Tiffany Haddish, actor, comedian, and author, Haddish shared her experience as a foster child. When she started using luggage instead of garbage bags, "[it was] like I had a purpose," she said, "like I'm a person, like I'm not garbage. I got this. It's mine, and my things are in here, and wherever I go I can take this with me, and I'm going somewhere." (Taggart, 2021)

I offered to return her tubs as soon as possible. She said it wasn't necessary, but I insisted. I needed an excuse for an opportunity to talk with her again and get information about the child I was bringing home with me.

While we were holding boxes and transferring the load in our now "properly selected" parking spots, Jackie told me a bit about herself. She was retired, the widow of a Mexican man, and spoke Spanish. *That's why she called me by my full name.* She only did respite care on weekends, a short-term placement to give current foster parents a temporary break (California Department of Social Services, 2021). She tried to be a grandmother to the children she hosted and keep in touch with them.

Jackie had known Lucy and her siblings since she was a toddler, when they first entered the system. This was the first time I was hearing about Lucy's seven-year-old brother and three-year-old sister and getting a sense of how long this girl had been in foster care. It seemed it had been at least a year and a half, maybe more. *The court could be close to deciding*, I thought. The goal is generally reunification with the biological family, but if that can't be achieved, the court strives for permanency, which means assigning a forever place for the child to call home. Courts generally drive for a case resolution. According to my friend Laura, from @foster. parenting on Instagram, the court may decide to terminate services anywhere between one to three years after the child enters the system, if reunification isn't possible. Based on the little information I was getting in those two or three minutes, and the fact she was having weekly visits with her parents, I pieced together she could be getting closer to reunification but wondered why she wasn't placed with her siblings.

It was a true gift I had those last five minutes with Jackie. She went a step further and gave me her cell phone number so we could get in touch once we had some privacy. I was grateful to get more insights about Lucy. It's often that the child's social worker also supports the bio parents in their reunification efforts, and therefore, they maintain confidentiality. The bio parents and kids feel enough shame as it is, without others digging into their private lives. Other times, the information is just unavailable. Consequently, foster parents are usually left in the dark with very limited information coming from the social worker. Nevertheless, more communication is imperative. Decisions are being made that will affect multiple people, and some key facts were missing in Lucy's case.

Weeks later, I found out the move to our house had been very sudden and Lucy cried the whole way to the Crisis Center. We were her fourth home within a year, as she had been removed from her prior two houses because she'd been aggressive to young kids, including her own sister. And by young, I mean a nine-year-old, older than both Lucy (five) and Gema (eight). I also learned too late that Lucy talked very graphically about the abuse she suffered from her dad, which was the reason she had to be removed from her preschool. Later, I would find myself in a position of having to give unplanned difficult explanations to Gema. I would have liked to know so I could have made a more informed decision on taking Lucy or I could have provided better care for her and my bio children. Sadly, it took months of discovery and heartache, all of which could have been avoided with more transparency. Don't they say sharing is caring? Well, in this case, it's true.

Once we finished moving all the boxes and tubs to my car, we walked toward Emily and Lucy. Lucy ran around the playground while Emily followed her trying to tell her I was her new foster mom, sharing details about my family and how Lucy was going to be much better in my house. It was clear Lucy didn't want to hear anything about it; she ran off the second she saw me coming, and I wondered how on earth she was going to voluntarily get in my car.

After a few attempts to slow Lucy down, Jackie told us all she was leaving. That was enough for Lucy to stop running and go after Jackie.

"Please don't leave me."

This was the first time I heard her voice. It was raspy, still the voice of a little girl, but she sounded older, weathered— very different from Gema's voice. Jackie gently told her she needed to leave while Lucy hung on to her legs and started crying. That's when Emily intervened and gently pulled her away and up into her arms.

"Hi, Lucy. I'm CarmenMaria. I know my name is long, so you can call me CM or Auntie. I will be taking you home. Everyone's excited to meet you," I said. She wouldn't budge. She didn't want to look at me or acknowledge my existence.

Right at that moment, Steve showed up with the kids. *Perfect timing,* I thought. We were hoping Gema would make Lucy feel safer. The air got lighter when I saw them. Gema was usually very good with younger children. Both her and Iago are welcoming, kind and thoughtful—except when it comes to each other, of course.

"Gema, help me open the door and start getting on your seat, please. When I bring Lucy in, please help me buckle her up, okay?" I asked. And I whispered, "She's very scared. Try to make her feel safe." She nodded.

Amid the commotion, Jackie put her sunglasses back on, waved quietly, and left. As she pulled out of the "loading-only" parking spot, she looked to see if there were no cars coming. I waited for her to look back at Lucy and wave goodbye, but she never did. She later shared she was crying and trying to hide it.

"C'mon Lucy, let's go. Do you want to walk on your own or do you want me to carry you to the car?" She extended her arms and held tight around my neck, sobbing into my blouse.

"It's okay. Everything is going to be okay," I said.

Gema was already grabbing the seat belt when I gently dropped this shaking little body on the pink booster seat.

In a matter of seconds, she was all buckled up asking Gema her name. Emily got close to my window, opened a smidgen, and said, "Bye, Lucy, I will stop by next week to check in and see how you're doing. Be good, okay?" And just like that, she turned around and headed back to the unwelcoming building. *Unfazed,* I thought.

I looked at the clock on my cell phone. It had been only fifteen minutes, and it felt I had received a lifetime of information and was left with a myriad of questions.

I took a deep breath, looked through the rear-view mirror, and asked "All buckled? Who wants McDonald's?"

CHAPTER 9

CHEETAH AND PUPPIES

DAY TWO

"We got a cheetah!" I responded when my mom called to check on our new little girl.

Our first night had been okay. She had a McDonald's Happy Meal with chicken nuggets, French fries, and apple juice on our way home. She ate it all. When we arrived, we explored the house. She ran up and down the stairs without saying a word, sprinting into each room while we tried to give a brief description in between breaths. Gema showed her the bathroom and the bedroom they would be sharing. Lucy sat quietly at the edge of her new bed. As I carried her heavy plastic tubs up the stairs, I started to think I wouldn't have enough space. I sat on the floor and asked her if she would like to help me unpack.

This is one of the most awkward moments when a child first arrives at your home. You have to take inventory of their clothes, and it's usually done in front of the child. If the children are old enough, a teenager for example, they sign the inventory list. This requirement helps ensure the child is receiving the clothing allowance and the foster family is spending the payment received to support the needs of the child (California HHS Agency, 2010). I understand the objective, but counting how many pairs of socks, underwear, t-shirts, pants they own and noting the conditions they're in, then having the child sign off on a list of their entire belongings... It's humiliating.

Before having Lucy, we did a few respite care and emergency placements: mostly preteens and teen girls whose foster parents needed a break, some in transition from one house to the next. I had to do the dreadful inventory. Each time I had a heavy weight in my stomach. It reminds me of those movies when they strip-search a criminal before booking them. From my perspective, it's a horrible invasion of privacy that highlights what little possessions foster kids have, and all they've lost.

In contrast with some kids who came with almost empty garbage bags, Lucy had *a lot* of clothes. I couldn't understand why she had so much. *How long has she been in the system to gather all this?* She had thirteen pairs of shoes, some new and unused sandals, and other shoes that were torn and clearly didn't fit her. As I folded every piece with care, I also noticed no one had thrown out or given away anything that didn't fit her. She had torn underwear, old and stained t-shirts, and various leopard-print items, including a short dress, an even shorter skirt, a jacket, and a shirt. At least most of it was clean. I held back the need to start separating what obviously didn't fit her, aware this could trigger a trauma response. An item I may give no value, that could have an unpleasant smell, like cigarettes or pot, can hold a memory or could be a gift from a bio parent. Unless it's necessary, I even try to hold off on laundry until I can get a better sense of what could upset the child.

It's been a learning process. I didn't think about so many considerations when we first started fostering, like the fact you can't give a haircut without the biological parents' permission. I've heard of other foster parents who had to go to court when the biological parent denied permission for a haircut.

It became clear not everything was going to fit in the dresser or the closet, so I decided to not unpack the heavy winter jacket and some of the summer clothes, including four new bathing suits (still with tags), alongside all the leopard-print outfits I personally disliked. They were too revealing for a five-year-old. I didn't know her love for cheetahs quite yet.

I opened a box with her toys. Several dolls were missing clothes, which I thought was ironic. She pulled out a very creepy doll in a velvety red-and-black dress and put it next to her bed on the floor, in perfect view for Gema, who feared dolls. In her words, "They give me the creeps." Gema kindly asked Lucy to put the doll in an area outside the bedroom where we also keep toys and explained dolls gave her nightmares. I knew Lucy heard Gema, but she turned toward the opposite wall, clearly ignoring the request. Gema looked at me, opening her eyes slightly, aware of the selective listening, and repeated her request a bit more firmly. I didn't realize then this small sign was a warning of future trouble. Later I would learn it wasn't a good idea for them to share a room.

I finally said, "Lucy, let's just leave the doll outside with the other toys please, so Gema is not scared at night. We can keep all your stuffies here though; those don't scare her."

I dreaded a meltdown because you never know what a request like this could prompt. Thank goodness she picked up all her dolls, including the creepy one, and took them outside to the play area, where we had cleared some bins for her toys.

It was late, but I still offered a shower or a bath, and she picked a bath. She was scared to be alone but didn't want anyone to help her, so I guarded the door in a way she could see my back, respecting her privacy but still offering protection. She put on pajamas and brushed her teeth with a new toothbrush, and I told her it was bedtime. She asked me to stay in the room with her, so I laid down on Gema's bed until she fell asleep, which was surprisingly fast. And just like that, we started our lives together.

~

"She hasn't talked much since she got here," I continued sharing with my mom. "I know it's just a day and a half, but the majority of the time she goes into a corner of the family room or sits on the edge of the sofa, holding her little stuffed tiger. When you get closer to her, she will attack. She hisses and tries to scratch. Yesterday she tried to bite me. She says she's a cheetah, a puppy, or a bear. I wish she could pick something less dangerous like a turtle or a bunny."

"Well, the first one hides and the second one procreates rapidly," said my mom. I never know if her comments are sarcastic or matter-of-fact. Maybe she was just trying to lighten up this tough situation.

"Remember when Danny used to be a puppy?" she prompted. The summer my parents spent with us in Chicago, they got to know Danny very well. My mom became especially fond of him. She has a memory of an elephant, so she would remember details like those.

"Oh my god, yes! It took him a few months to be human. But he never hurt us. Lucy tries to scratch us, and it's mostly when Gema is nearby," I said. At that moment, I remembered when Danny used to run on four legs and put his tongue out like a puppy. He barked and turned onto his back so we could scratch his belly. It was both funny and weird. I didn't recall any of my permanent kids (bio or step) ever acting like animals, but who knows? Maybe they had, and I forgot all about it. Danny never played aggressively though.

"Just give her time. She needs to feel safe to be a human. You can also ask her why she is an animal and what each of them means. Maybe she will just tell you," my mom said wisely.

So I did. I asked Lucy many times until she finally shared the meaning of each animal. They were her protectors. And after about three months she stopped becoming them, but not before the cheetah showed up and scratched Gema on the belly.

I feared this couldn't be undone later and the relationship would become irreparable.

I wasn't wrong.

CHAPTER 10

THE ER

DAY THREE

I spent all Saturday with Lucy at the ER.

That poor baby. She was in so much distress. Later, I would piece together what happened.

Lucy shared how she was "kicked out" of Mrs. Lenora's house (her prior foster mother) and Jackie (her transport) confirmed how unexpected it felt. Back then, I thought it was very poorly handled, but knowing what I know now, I can empathize.

Mrs. Lenora had put in the fourteen-day notice, because Lucy kept misbehaving, throwing tantrums, unbuckling herself out of her booster seat in the middle of the highway, and hitting the nine-year-old in the house, none of which was shared with us. Once she put in her notice, the social worker found Lucy a home (ours) faster than anticipated. I don't know if Mrs. Lenora had time to regret her decision, but once you give notice, it's like starting a chain reaction. It's all fast and unstoppable. When I chatted over the phone with Mrs. Lenora a few months after Lucy came to us, she shared she didn't have the heart to face her and say goodbye, so she sent her to school as if it was any other normal day. That afternoon, Jackie picked her up with her clothes and all her toys in the car and told her she was going to a new house.

That's how Lucy realized she was not returning to Mrs. Lenora's home that evening. She interpreted it as if she was kicked out of her house because of "a little mistake," which meant she hit the nine-year-old badly while Mrs. Lenora was driving.

But I didn't know any of that and we hadn't experienced hosting a child with that level of trauma, so the ER trip came as a complete surprise.

The first and second nights were relatively good. The only real nuisance was I had to keep her company the whole time. She didn't want to be left alone for one second. I couldn't go to the bathroom without her being outside the door, literally like a puppy. The cheetah was annoying but when redirected, I was surprised to see how compliant she was with the rules. It seems naive, but I thought she was adapting well. On Fridays, we do pizza and movie night. She helped make her own pizza, and we watched *Monsters, Inc.* I know there is a honeymoon period, but this was better than what we had experienced back in Chicago with Danny on his first nights watching *Wreck-it-Ralph*.

Could it be this smooth? Are kids really this resilient?

That Saturday, she came into my room at about 6:30 a.m., and as soon as I opened my eyes to say hi, she started throwing up. Right there, on me, on my pajamas, on the bed and next to the bed, on the carpet. *Everywhere.* I didn't even have enough time to get a bucket and clean up the first round of vomit when the next started. At first, I thought it was the pizza from the night before, so I wasn't too worried. But when she wouldn't stop, I decided to call my social worker, Shonna.

Shonna wouldn't pick up, and I kept calling in between vomits. It kept going to voicemail. I didn't know what to do. In those moments you forget all your training. I'm not talking about foster care training; I'm talking about the real-life experience of being a mom. So I called the emergency line for the agency, and Jerry, the regional head of the agency whom I had rarely interacted with, picked up. I was so glad we worked with an agency and someone is on call at all times!

"Give her some Pedialyte, but if she doesn't stop throwing up, you will have to take her to the ER because you don't want her to get dehydrated. Do you have her medical card?" asked Jerry.

I didn't have her medical card, and I was embarrassed I didn't. I should have known what to do when kids throw up. I should have also asked for the medical card when I picked her up. More importantly, I felt silly thinking Lucy liked us and was adapting well. I was wrong on so many levels.

Through this process, I've learned transitions from a foster home into a new home can be as traumatic, equivalent to when they're first removed from their parents' home. "Failure to transition properly jeopardizes the child's continued ability to attach to anyone... there will inevitably be trauma when the child is moved to a different day-to-day caregiver, especially when the child has formed an attachment to the current caregiver" (Advokids, 2022).

And the trauma came gushing out in a nasty liquid form.

We decided to head to the ER, and I got a bucket for the back seat. It was five minutes away, but in that time she threw up twice—once in the bucket and again in the parking lot. At least not on the car itself.

COVID protocols were in place, and we had to wait outside of the building, six feet from the few people checking in.

It was cold early that morning. An apathetic male employee sat on a chair at a portable desk with a laptop outside of the main ER entrance checking people in. Lucy got tired, so she let me hold her when we went to the front of the line. I was surprised at how heavy she felt.

"Good morning. What happened?" the employee asked, looking at the keyboard.

"She's been throwing up nonstop since early this morning."

"First name and last name?" He still did not look up.

"Give me one second," I said.

He raised his head and finally looked at me from behind the double mask. "You don't know her name?" he inquired a little too loudly. One nurse standing inside the building turned around to look at us.

I blushed as I tried to hold Lucy with one arm without dropping her, almost an impossible task. I tried to pull her paperwork out of my backpack with my free hand, hoping Jerry had talked to Shonna and I had the insurance card waiting for me in my emails.

"Well, her name is Lucy."

"Last name?" he asked, annoyed.

"Please give me one second," I said, while trying to get my backpack's zipper unstuck. "She just came to our care a couple of days ago," I whispered.

"I can't hear you with the mask on," he said considerably louder than earlier.

"She is our new foster daughter and came to live with us just two nights ago," I repeated, also louder than what I intended.

Lucy projectile vomited over my shoulder, into the grass next to the sidewalk. Luckily not on me, although the smell was overpowering.

The nurse, who overheard us, walked to me, handed me some wipes, and said gently, "Let me help you with her." She took Lucy to a chair next to the entrance. I checked my cell phone for messages. *No insurance.* I pulled out the paperwork and tried to respond to all the usual questions any mother should know.

When was the last time she ate? What had she eaten? Did she have any medical conditions? Any allergies? Was she on any medication? Any medical history they should be aware of? Who was her primary care physician?

I don't know. I don't know. I don't know. She just came to us. I don't know. I don't know.

I should know, but I don't know.

"Insurance, please."

"The insurance card should be coming any second," I replied embarrassingly.

At least I had the paperwork that said she was in the custody of the state and the foster care agreement stating she was in our care. And even though we didn't have her insurance card, the hospital searched for her Medicaid number and found it. We were in!

~

We spent the full day trying for Lucy to pee in a cup, getting her to take anti-nausea medication, getting a blood sample, cleaning up the vomit on me, trying to vomit while hugging the toilet in a *very* dirty restroom of a *very* public emergency room *during a pandemic.* After hours of waiting for the lab work, the doctor came out and told me Lucy had *nothing.* All tests were normal. She was just *a bit* dehydrated.

"It seems she may just be a little nervous. Other than that, she's in perfect health. I'll bring you the discharge papers and you should be able to go home soon," she said.

"That's it?" I asked.

"That's it... keep up the good work, Mamma. She's fine," she said as she walked away.

I'm not her mamma, and she's not fine. If I was her mamma, I would know all the answers and she wouldn't be here. She's been throwing up all day. She's NOT FINE. Kids are resilient bullshit! She was pulled out of her prior home, and she was placed in a house with strangers. She's a brave little one, and she's trying to hold it together, but she's clearly not fine.

"It's time to go, sweetie. We will get home and take a warm bath. Maybe we can eat something and then go to bed," I told Lucy while I offered my arms to hold her.

And she accepted me. I lifted her and she put her arms around my neck tightly, like a baby, like a fifty-six-pound baby, and we headed toward the car while I tried not to drop her.

She was exhausted. I was exhausted. But somehow, over vomit, pee, and blood samples, we bonded. Perhaps she was going to be fine. And maybe that's how "mammas" are born.

CHAPTER 11

MORNINGS

DAY FOUR

I woke up feeling someone was looking at me.

Yes. Lucy was standing next to my bed, staring at me in her purple nightgown. Her little body was shaking. I looked at her and looked at the time on my cell phone: 5:27 a.m. *Fuck*, I thought. We had such a long day yesterday in the ER. *Can't she just be tired and go to sleep?*

"It's really early, sweetheart. Why don't you go to your bed and go back to sleep?" I said.

She shook her head.

"Are you okay?" I asked.

She shook her head again.

"Are you scared?"

She nodded.

"Do you want to crawl into bed with me?" I asked, hoping she would say yes and lie down next to me and I could go back to sleep. I didn't think if it was against our foster care training recommendations or not.

She shook her head.

Okay, so now what? I need to sleep. I surrendered and sat up.

"How can I help you?" I asked.

"I need to go potty."

"You can go here if you want," I said, pointing at the en suite bathroom.

"I'm scared. Can you come with me and stand outside?" she replied.

"Sure thing." *Darn, I'm so tired. I really need to sleep. I hope this improves soon.*

DAY SIXTEEN

I woke up with the familiar feeling Lucy was standing next to me. I opened my eyes slightly. Yep, Lucy was there. It had become her daily habit. She just stared.

She was next to my bed in her not-so-new, light blue, Elsa-from-*Frozen* nightgown. Steve got it for her the week before, and she hadn't taken it off. *I will need to figure out how to wash that soon.*

I looked at her, then looked at my cell phone to check the time: 6:06 a.m. *Still early, but at least we're past six. I have a meeting at 7:30 a.m. today, so it won't hurt to wake up early.* I just wished I had gone to bed earlier, but bedtimes were rough. I had to split between Gema and Lucy, considering they weren't getting along despite all our efforts, and each needed individual attention.

I was doing a good job finishing work at around 6 p.m., which was earlier than usual. Steve had dinner ready at about 6:15 p.m. Two dinners, actually: one for Lucy and one for the rest of us, since she never liked what we made. After eating, Gema, Lucy, and I picked up the family room, while Iago and

Steve cleaned the kitchen, and I headed upstairs to prepare Lucy's shower.

And then, every night, the same ordeal.

Lucy took hours in the shower, with the running water, playing, washing her hair, which was down past her waist. When she would finally come out and get her pajamas on, we still needed to watch a short TV show while I brushed her hair and teeth, potty time, bedtime games, meditation music. And then she would be ready to sleep. But because she was afraid to sleep alone, I ended up staying there until she fell asleep, most nights past 9 p.m.

That wouldn't have been too bad if Gema's bedtime wasn't at nine, but by then, she hadn't spent any time with me, so we pushed her bedtime to later. I started her routine at 9 p.m., and we finished at about ten. She didn't need much help, but she complained it was just too fast and she hadn't spent any time with me. I ended up exhausted every night. And it was taking a toll on her too. Although it was only one hour later, she couldn't fall asleep right away. Mornings were becoming increasingly more difficult for everyone.

"It's really early, sweetheart. Why don't you go to your bed and go back to sleep? Remember 'wakey' time is not until 7:30 on weekdays," I said. I had added to our vocabulary "wakey" versus "sleepy" time.

"It's not 7:30 yet?" she asked.

"Nope," I replied. "Do you want to crawl into the bed with me?" *Please say yes, so I can sleep in a bit longer.*

She shook her head. I wasn't surprised.

"How can I help you?" I asked, not wanting to sit up.

"I need to go potty. Can you come with me and stand outside?"

"I think we can start going potty alone. This house is safe. Remember?" I said while my body was fighting to get out of bed and my eyelids felt like they weighed a thousand tons.

"Okay, but can you please come?" she answered.

"Okay, but remember this house is safe," I repeated as I dragged myself out of bed. I was so tired, and I sat outside the bathroom while she went. *We can't continue having these early mornings and the long bedtime routines.*

"Don't forget to wash your hands," I reminded.

"I know," she answered.

I'm exhausted. Eventually, this has to get better.

CHAPTER 12

THE ZOO VISIT

DAY THIRTY-ONE

"Are you brave enough to see cheetahs?" My question was directed to Steve, not Lucy.

We had been debating if we could handle Lucy outside the house and do a family day as California opened up from the pandemic. I wasn't sure if I was brave enough, but we decided to try.

We thought we were the first ones to give this experience to Lucy, but she told us she had already been at the zoo with her prior foster mother. And so, I told her this was a better zoo. This one had cheetahs, bears, and sloths—the first one being Lucy's favorite animal and the last one being Gema's.

Lucy had shared she had been "kicked out" of all prior homes, and I kept thinking that wouldn't happen with us. No matter what, she would stay in our home until she went back to her mom's. I wondered if that was what her prior foster mother felt too and if that's what we *all* feel—that with us, things would work out and we are better, more prepared, more resilient, more caring than prior foster homes. That you will be their hero. I wanted to be the best foster parent this child could have.

The excitement leading up to the visit kept building, and that morning she woke up, and instead of staring at me, she got ready on her own without asking for help. When I came downstairs, she had even filled her water bottle. Not even the ninety-minute drive fazed her.

I had pre-purchased tickets online, but that line was still long. Lucy was getting impatient, so I looked over to check if the "members-only line" was shorter and if the cost was manageable compared to the regular-price tickets. It was, so we switched to the membership line and zoomed right up to the first window in no time.

"We are coming to see the cheetahs," Lucy said to the nice old lady wearing a volunteer tag at the counter.

"And sloths," said Gema. "Don't forget we came to see the sloths first." I nodded while I put my index finger on my mouth, gently saying "shh" to both.

"Hope you enjoy your visit, hon," the woman said to Lucy only, ignoring Gema. She then turned to me. "Are you a current member or do you want to become a member?"

"Hi. We would like to become members; it seems it's a worthwhile deal," I responded, wishing she had looked at Gema as well.

"I'm so glad. Your kids will enjoy it very much. You will need to fill in this form. How many children under the age of eighteen do you have in the household?"

"Three," I said, and Lucy quickly added, "I'm not her kid. She's not my mom. I have a real mommy, and she's waiting for me at home. None of them are my real family."

That woman's facial expression immediately changed. Her kind smile disappeared, and she looked at me with serious concern. I didn't know who else had heard. *Did I bring the paperwork where it says she's my foster child? Is she going to put out an Amber Alert because she thinks I kidnapped Lucy? Where is my social worker's phone number? Where's my phone? Does she have one of those red buttons under her desk where a SWAT team will show up instantly?*

"Oh sweetie, you know while you're with us, you are part of our family. And yes, your real mommy is working very hard so you can all go back. But for now, you're part of our family," I said awkwardly.

To make matters worse, Lucy said, "I have told you many, many, many times. Do not call me *sweetie*. Call me Lucy."

"Sorry, Lucy," I said. I clarified for the zoo volunteer, "She's our new foster daughter, and we are all still adapting."

And there it was, the answer I hear constantly, and I cringe every time: "Oh, what a wonderful thing to do. It is very, very kind what you and your family are doing for this poor girl. She's so lucky to have you. You are a saint. Let me see if I can give you a discount."

"Oh, it's okay. It's not necessary, really. No, thank you," I said uncomfortably.

Now I regret not having said something different. I don't know what I should have said exactly, but maybe I should have defended Lucy and told this woman she was not a lucky girl; there was nothing lucky about the situation. Instead, I froze and didn't say anything because I knew it was well intended. But it's just weird when other people tell us we're doing a wonderful thing for these kids. It's especially difficult if the child is standing next to you—as if Lucy had not gone through enough. Foster kids, or any children for that matter, should never feel they're someone's charity mission.

And the mixed feelings... I was not her real mom. Of course I wasn't. I was not trying to replace her biological mom, but I was her mom for that period. And hearing it said so directly hurt me. *I'm trying so hard to bond with you, baby girl, and calling you sweetie is part of it.*

I took a deep breath and reminded myself this woman's intentions were good and Lucy was hurting. It wasn't personal.

"Do you have a map, please? And could you please show me where the cheetahs and the sloths are located?" I asked.

"Oh... unfortunately our sloths died, and we don't have cheetahs anymore. They got moved to another zoo to see if they could mate," she whispered. She added, "But we have many monkeys, jaguars, and lions."

NOOOOOO!

Although Steve and I tried to share the similarities, "wild feline" was too broad of a term, and jaguars are *not* cheetahs. We had a harder time trying to convince Gema monkeys were more interesting than sloths because they move faster and interact more. She insisted animals with so many fingers don't compare with cute two-toed or three-toed sloths. Thank goodness Iago is always "chill." As a good teen boy, he was happy as long as he was fed!

So we pulled an old trick: ice cream. Dippin' Dots was a success—expensive and messy, but a success. And at the end of the day, we even fed the giraffes, not with ice cream, obviously. That moment was amazing. Everyone was excited, laughing nervously, bonding. Not everything ended up being a disappointment.

It feels as parents, we're constantly trying to compensate for missed expectations. When the older kids were little and Steve shared custody with their mom, he tried to pack everything he hadn't done in a full school year in the short summer we had them. Dozens of activities and experiences concentrated in a few weeks. And with our foster kids, we try to compensate for their past pain by providing them with love and experiences as well, as if it will somehow diminish what they went through, knowing it's not possible. I find it's similar with our own biological kids. Is there something extra we can do for them? Because we know they're giving up so much sharing their parents' time and their space.

And while the zoo visit didn't meet anyone's expectations, it ended up being pretty good for a family day with a family that wasn't Lucy's *real* one.

CHAPTER 13

NIGHTS

DAY THIRTY-SIX

It had been a few nights since I realized our bedtime routine had become easier. Don't get me wrong. It still took hours, but I think Lucy and I started having fun together.

"Was that a small time?" she asked, referring to how long her shower took.

"That was pretty good; it was only twenty minutes. Not bad at all." It was true, compared to the forty-five to sixty minutes she took when she first came home.

"Yay! I did it! I did it!" she sang really loudly.

"Yes, you did it! Now PJs and teeth," I replied, trying to keep the momentum going.

"You forgot my hair, silly!" and she laughed.

"I'm silly. I forgot! Let me brush your hair," I said, and she put on her PJ's and sat in front of me, on my bed, while I turned on one of her favorite cartoons. I was thankful she had learned how to use hair conditioner, because her hair was very long, and it took a solid thirty minutes to brush it.

"Let's count. When I say three, two, one, we start, okay?" she asked before brushing her teeth. She had convinced me we had to compete in a contest in which whoever brushed their teeth better, won. She would always win...

"How do you know you won?" I would ask every night.

"I just know!" she would reply and immediately opened her mouth in a grin, showing me her teeth. She was missing a front tooth, which I had saved to give to her mom on our next visit.

After hair, teeth, and TV watching, it was bedtime. She would whistle—like a grown man—or sing beautifully on her way to the bedroom, while doing cartwheels. Quite a multitasker if you think about it.

"Can you stay more than five minutes please?" Five minutes was for when I put her in time out (or time in, since I sat next to her), following the rule of one minute per year of age. It was soon going to be six minutes, since her birthday was the upcoming weekend. I laughed but didn't correct her, and it was *never* less than forty minutes at bedtime.

"We have to play Name Five! No! Let's play I Spy," she said, as she crawled into bed. I had learned not to play truth or dare at night because she always wanted me to pick *dare* and would ask me to do jumping jacks.

"I spy with my little eye someone with brown hair." She smiled without looking at me.

"Me!"

"Yes! Your turn."

"I spy with my little eye someone kind, beautiful, smart, brave, and strong!"

"Me!"

"How did you know?" I asked, faking being serious.

She laughed, tickled me, and said, "You're the tickle lettuce."

"And you are the tickle tomato!" We both giggled, hugged, and tickled some more.

"Time's up! Good night. I love you, baby," I said while looking at the time, feeling guilty I was missing time with Gema, but enjoying every second of our developing relationship.

"I love you too, tickle lettuce," she replied, giving me a long hug.

This became our bedtime routine. And it kept extending and extending, in part because she insisted and in part because sometimes those were the only good moments of the day and I wanted to enjoy them. I was making a connection, and she was trusting me and healing, little by little.

However, I was oblivious to how spending more time with Lucy was impacting Gema.

CHAPTER 14

BECOMING MAMMA

DAY FORTY-THREE

It was 6:30 a.m., and my eyes were wide open.

Lucy's daily early stares were changing my natural sleep schedule, and I was becoming a morning person. I guess fostering changes a lot more than your heart.

Even from behind closed doors, I could hear her little feet running in the distance. She was loud! She was loud in everything she did. Her voice, her steps, her whistles, her whole presence. Her regular volume was many more decibels than I was used to, even when we had all six kids around. She didn't talk, really; she yelled.

I was on a conference call with a co-worker once, and he heard Lucy in the background. She was being loud, as always.

"I guess they never paid any attention to her. That's maybe why she feels the need to yell instead of talking," he said.

Oh, wow. Based on her Monday therapy sessions, I knew she had been abused, but *ignored*? That hadn't even occurred to me, but it made total sense.

I remembered my previous foster care class. Jerry, the head of our agency for our region, had introduced us to Dr.

Karyn Purvis' work, who is one of the founders of the Institute of Child Development and the co-creator of Trust-Based Relational Intervention (TBRI). Any parent—biological, step, or foster—should take her training. Jerry quoted her to a child: "Abuse means *I don't like you*. But neglect... being ignored... it's much worse. It means *you don't exist.*"

I realized Lucy had been both abused *and* neglected.

Lucy's steps got closer and closer. I had started to close my bedroom door at night thinking that may deter her from entering in the mornings. But no. Nothing deterred her. As she swung the door open without knocking, I closed my eyes and faked I was asleep. She tapped my shoulder, and I jumped. I didn't expect her to touch me.

This time she spoke first: "Sorry."

"It's okay baby, but what have we said about respecting people and not touching them? Especially when they're asleep?"

"I forgot," she replied.

"It's still before 'wakey' time. Not 7:30 yet, so what's up, *amor*?"

What could it be this time? It had been a few weeks since she had been going to the bathroom alone, which was tremendous progress. Other things hadn't improved much. Bedtime was still long for both girls, and Gema was becoming very vocal about how much she was struggling with Lucy. Lucy was not only clamoring for more attention from both of us parents but had also learned to push every one of Gema's buttons.

In turn, Gema started demanding much more attention, saying she missed me and every time she tried to be with me, Lucy interrupted us. "You don't spend time with me anymore, *Mami*," she would repeat.

So I started bedtime routines earlier, but the duration only extended, and I was finishing even later. I had no time for Iago, Steve, or anything else anymore. Lucy was absorbing as much of me as she could.

"Do you need to go potty?" I asked, hoping we hadn't regressed.

"No, I already went," she replied.

Amazing! Hope she washed her hands, but I'm not going to ask.

"What is it, *amor*?" I sighed, starting to get a bit annoyed.

"Can I get into your bed?" she asked hesitantly.

WHAT! This is new! And what's the rule for this?

This is the hardest thing. When they're little, what do you do? You still need to teach them they shouldn't crawl into bed with adults, but you also want to hug and cuddle with them. I had to remember to ask Shonna what is recommended.

I moved next to Steve, putting myself in the middle of the bed so Lucy could lie just next to me. *I hope Gema doesn't wake up now and see this. She'll flip.* There wasn't enough physical space in the bed for all of us.

"Hop on," I said. "Ouch! Careful!" I exclaimed; she had literally jumped on top of me, and her knee hit my ribs.

"Sorry," she said and giggled. "Sorry, Mamma."

My heart stopped for a second. The butterflies rose in the pit of my stomach. She called me "Auntie," "tickle lettuce," and "hey." This was the first time she used "Mamma."

"It's okay, baby," I said, not knowing how else to respond or what to think. She had told me so many times I wasn't her mommy.

She cleared it up for me.

"Until I go back to my real mommy, you're my mamma. Because you're the mommy of this house, so you're my mamma when I'm here." She giggled, grabbed my arm wrapping it around her, snuggled, and closed her eyes.

I prayed Gema didn't wake up and find us, and I hoped the distance between those two wouldn't become even larger. I dreaded the consequences.

But the moment felt so precious I wanted to savor it for as long as it lasted without feeling guilty about my own child.

Because this one was my child too. I put her to bed every night, wiped her tears when she cried, helped her with bath time, brushed her hair, kept her safe, and loved her. Steve and I were raising her. She was becoming ours. And as I closed my eyes next to her, I wished those minutes would never end. I was her mamma.

CHAPTER 15

MAKEUP

———

Trigger warning: graphic content and sexual violence

DAY FIFTY-EIGHT

"Do you want me to do your makeup, Mamma?" Lucy asked on a Sunday afternoon.

No, not really. I thought. *I can't do it again. I can't learn more.*

The prior Sunday, she did my makeup, and it ended in the most emotionally disturbing night I could've ever imagined.

~

It was before bedtime. She had been very hyper all day, and brushing her hair after the shower, usually soothing, wasn't accomplishing much. That's why when she asked if she could do my makeup, in an attempt to calm her down, I let her.

Makeup usually did the trick. She was meticulous about it. She "worked" silently, reminding me of people who go into a deep meditation state. She would cover the small table I kept in a corner of my bedroom with tissues. "In case I mess up, Mamma," she would say. Then, she would bring *all* my makeup and organize it on the table. She would grab a brush and add an insane amount of blush or eyeshadow. She always started with the foundation, went to the eyes, moved to the lips, and finished with the blush. This six-year-old girl knew very well the "theory" of applying makeup and was very proud of her own knowledge. But the result was never pretty. I most definitely looked like a clown almost every time.

That night, I asked a bit sarcastically if she liked clowns. Lucy's body started shaking unexpectedly, her eyes teared up, and she crawled into a fetal position.

"What's happening, baby? It's okay, you're safe here." This had become my default answer: *It's okay, you're safe here.*

I rubbed her back. "Do you not like clowns?"

She shook her head.

"You are okay, baby. Do you want to talk about it?"

"I'm scared of Pennywise. He's always in my nightmares. I try to forget him, but he always tries to get me." Her voice was shaking as much as her little body.

Who the heck is Pennywise? With my free hand, I reached out to grab my phone and searched. It turns out he's the main character of the horror movie *IT*, based on Stephen King's novel. R-rated. I hate horror movies. When I was a kid, I had nightmares just from watching an ad.

"I see. Yes, I would be scared too, but he's not real, sweetheart."

"My bubba said he's real." She rarely mentioned her brother, but when she did, she called him "Bubba."

"Your brother probably thought he was real, but he's not real. I promise. I know it's scary. That's why some movies are only for grown-ups. We don't want to watch them because sometimes we can get nightmares." This is always hard. It's that fine line of not criticizing the biological parents and her life before us, trying to not make her feel guilty about it, while teaching her how some things should be different.

"I know... my bubba loves scary movies. He made me watch Pennywise many times."

"I'm sorry about that. Where were your mom and dad when you were watching that movie?" *Many times? Where were her parents?* This is where it was difficult for me to be neutral, because her brother must have been five and she must have been three when they were watching an R-rated horror movie.

She suddenly stopped shaking, stood up, and giggled. "They were asleep. They like to sleep after they get naked and kiss. They touch their privates, and they make funny noises."

My heart raced, and at that point, how could I *not* be concerned? I needed to mentally register everything I was hearing, since as a mandated reporter—a requirement of every foster parent—I had to document and share all the facts accurately with our social worker.

"I see, and how come you know this?" I asked, trying to not let my feelings get in the way. My questions needed to be open-ended, carefully crafted to avoid putting words in her mouth or to even have the perception I was leading her to specific answers.

"Oh, we all slept there. In the same room. My bubba, my sissy, and I, we all sleep on the floor next to Daddy and Mommy."

"Aww... well, I'm glad in this house we have more space so the girls can sleep in one room, Iago in another, and the parents in another." How else was I supposed to respond? I was mentally going through all the training where they said we need to ensure we're not judgmental, that we should listen. Maybe there was a reason... I was hoping it was accidental.

"Yeah, I like this house. We have a lot of bathrooms too. I like Steve uses the bathroom alone."

I didn't know where her comment was going, but I wanted to use the opportunity to educate a bit about boundaries, in the same way I've been sharing this with my own kids since they were little. "Yes, that's good. If there is only one bathroom in the house, we need to take turns. We don't need to be in the bathroom at the same time grown-ups or the other kids are there."

"Except Steve or Iago," she said.

"No. Steve and Iago don't need to be in the bathroom at the same time as you. They can use another bathroom, or they can wait. No boys need to be in the same bathroom with you." I kept thinking about her counter arguments. I could hear her saying, *What if it's my bubba or Daddy?*

"Yeah... I know," she said. Her answer surprised me, but she added, "Do you want to know my story?"

I nodded.

She continued, "I was in the bathroom when my daddy was taking showers, and one day, he asked me to suck his privates. I told him I didn't want to, but he said please. I said no, but he said pretty please. And he says when someone says pretty please, you *have* to say yes. So I said okay. But I didn't like it, Mamma. He peed in my mouth and on the floor. It was disgusting."

The world paused. I was appalled. My mind tried to comprehend what I just heard. My heart pounded trying to rip itself out of my chest and escape. I was nauseated and lightheaded, as if I'd received a full blow to the head. *I can't throw up right now. What should I say? How do I respond?*

They don't teach you how to react to something like this. Not being judgmental, my fucking ass! How can I NOT react to this? How come that criminal of a father isn't in jail? How come she has to see him EVERY week? What's wrong with the system? Why is he still working toward reunification? Don't they know? Yes, they have to know because she goes every week to group therapy for sexually abused children. They do know! If they know, why does she see him every week? I have to say something.

Those few seconds felt like centuries, but I pulled myself together and responded, "I'm sorry, baby. I'm really sorry. You're a very brave girl for telling me. Thank you for sharing. And I want you to know that wasn't your fault, sweetie."

"Yes, it was my fault. I said yes. I said no first, but he said pretty please so I said yes. It was just a little mistake. He didn't know what he was doing; it's not his fault." She looked down as she spoke.

"It's not your fault, baby. Even if you said yes. You can say yes many, many times, and it's still not your fault. Grown-ups know what they're doing. Kids may not know. But grown-ups know."

"He hasn't said sorry. You have to say sorry if you make a mistake, but he hasn't said sorry. I tell him to say sorry. When I see him, I say, 'You need to say sorry,' but he doesn't."

"Does he say anything?"

"That he's working on it."

"And are you okay with that?" It was probably unnecessary for me to stir her emotions further, but I couldn't help it. I was beside myself by then, and I was holding back my rage and shock as best as I could.

"No," she replied immediately.

"Have you told anyone this? Have you told your social worker?"

"No, I keep forgetting. Can you tell her? Can we record it like a movie? So I don't forget to tell her"

I didn't want to miss the chance to get proof against her abuser. I grabbed my cell phone and started recording. Like a movie... Like a horror movie. The type that will give anyone eternal nightmares.

It took a while. She wanted to keep trying and get it "perfect." She would say, "Cut, let's start over," right before she would share the abuse, and I had to start over. Before the second take, I told her we didn't have to film it and I could just let the social worker know, but she insisted, "Let's just make this movie." And with every take, she decided to add things to her outfit. She added a necklace with take two, another necklace and a bracelet with take three, then a purse and a jacket. She put her hair up in a ponytail, then let her hair down. But she didn't want to stop. On her final take, she increased her pitch and said, "Hi, I'm your cousin Lucy." *Your cousin?* I don't pretend to understand the disassociation she was having, but it was heartbreaking to see how she was becoming a character in full costume with every take. A caricature. No. A clown.

By the end of that grueling recording, I was exhausted. She was exhausted. But she slept that night.

At least one of us did.

I wasn't prepared for that. Not even a thousand more hours of training would have prepared me for it. How could anyone be the same after hearing that? When I showed the recording to her social worker, Emily, although she knew about it, she wasn't ready to see it either. But this is the reality of foster care, the reality of children who have been sexually abused, the reality of children being trafficked. We need to know about it. We need to share it, so people know how bad it is. So we can do better. So we can get them help earlier, prevent them from going back, give foster families better response training, and get counseling for everyone.

Despite my concerns about having more revelations during makeup sessions, we started having them every Sunday. She felt safe, and we bonded over them. I even let her use my light pink lipstick occasionally. She would look at her reflection on my full-size mirror, smile, and say, "I look like you, Mamma."

I would always reply, "You look like you, baby. You are brave and beautiful. I love you."

CHAPTER 16

UNGROOMING

**If you know anyone being trafficked
or if you need help, reach out to:
National Human Trafficking Hotline
Call: 1 (888) 373-7888
Or SMS: 233733 (Text "HELP" or "INFO")
Website: http://humantraffickinghotline.org**

or

**If you believe a child isn't trafficked, but may
be missing or exploited, please call the:
National Center for Missing & Exploited
Children, twenty-four hours a day at
1-800-THE-LOST (1-800-843-5678)**

Some days, especially after visits with *him*, Lucy would throw massive tantrums.

We knew tantrums were due to happen. We'd been taught about how trauma affects the brain of children and how children with trauma develop unhealthy behaviors. They could be aggressive or defiant, and it's difficult to predict what could trigger them (Adopt Us Kids, 2022). It could be an item of clothing, the way something was said, a smell, a sound, a song, a question. We were prepared to document and learn the patterns. We were trained and ready.

Or so we thought.

Generally speaking, we all know the theory is different from the practice. But it's hard to not be internally rattled and feel incompetent when things are flying at you. Or when the kid you love is yelling, throwing LEGOs, dolls, a metal unknown object on your face. When an otherwise sweet girl is biting, kicking, hitting, and insulting you with words you didn't even know existed. Or when a child kicked so hard the newly decorated Christmas tree comes down, shattering the beautiful ornaments that remind you of home.

It was devastating to see how much Lucy was hurting and even harder to see the glaring patterns after seeing her dad. It was beyond frustrating knowing I was unable to prevent them.

Monday court-mandated visits with her dad became traumatic for everyone. Lucy had either epic tantrums or sexualized behaviors, such as humping on the couch, trying to rub her butt on Steve or Iago, or trying to put her hands inside Steve's shorts. She was so small though her bottom barely reached Steve's knees, who's six feet, two inches. Every time it happened, we sent an email to her social worker, and added it to the larger document we were compiling as evidence, which we turned in to our Child Family Team (CFT) monthly meeting.

I wasn't ready to keep an impartial attitude. I was furious at the father, and I had to make Herculean efforts to appear neutral in front of Lucy.

In addition to redirecting her with each incident, we also had to talk with our kids right after to somehow explain to Iago Lucy didn't really know what she was doing when she tried to touch him. We had to explain to Gema sometimes grown-ups do things that are *that* wrong. I was even less prepared for the follow-up questions: "But how come he's not in jail?" from Iago or "Why did her dad do that to her?" from Gema.

When I thought it couldn't get any worse, Lucy would randomly share more details of what her dad did. Or she would repeat "her story" after a shower or after a visit. In the same sentence, she would say how much she loved her "daddy," missed him, and wanted to go back home, as well as how mad she really was.

"I want to tell him I'm really mad. I want him to say, 'I'm sorry,'" she would say before immediately adding, "but it's not his fault. He didn't know what he was doing. I miss my daddy. He's the best daddy in the world!"

And I responded very consistently, "He knew what he was doing. All grown-ups know."

As the weeks and months went by, Lucy kept going to therapy and seeing her dad. She continued demonstrating these post-visit behaviors, which lasted for a couple of days. We barely had "down" days between visits. We documented, sent reports to the social workers, talked with her clinicians, but I felt no progress was being made. He was still seeing Lucy, and she still thought it was her fault.

Steve brought her home one day after her session with her dad. She gave me a huge hug and said, "Look, Mamma!" pointing at a colorful bead necklace with the letters L-U-C-Y, each one in a different color.

"Oh, that's pretty. And it has your name on it!" I said, thinking Steve must have gotten it for her. I hoped he had gotten one for Gema too.

"Yes, my daddy and I made it together. He loves me and he says he's trying very hard to get me back."

He's grooming her! And was no one noticing? I was infuriated by what I perceived to be a lack of action from the system.

Maybe people don't realize this could be happening because it's unthinkable and no one in their sound mind would even think a father could do that. The definition is not even accurate in the *Merriam-Webster Dictionary*! It says:

groom
verb
groomed; grooming; grooms
Definition of *groom, transitive verb*
1. to clean and maintain the appearance [...] *Nope, not this one.*
2. to make neat or attractive [...] *Not this one either.*
3. to get into readiness for a specific objective: Prepare [...] *Not quite.*

According to the Polaris Project, grooming is the process in which traffickers find those moments when people are vulnerable, working the angles, manipulating reality, and leveraging fears. It is methodical and intentional, and it works.

Evilelove has a much better definition in *The Urban Dictionary:*

Groom: when a sexual or other kind of predator sets the stage for abusing another, such as a child or other person [...]

May give toys and/or other gifts and favors to the intended victim to gain trust [...]

Yes! He was building her trust again with toys and presents, taking advantage of how deeply she loved him. She defended him, excused him, blamed herself, missed him, and wanted to go back to how things were. She didn't recognize any of it as his fault because she had said "yes."

This is *exactly* how pedophiles groom kids. I've read horrific stories of sex-trafficked youth in my course at Foster Parent College. Pedophiles provide attention and gifts, and they manipulate vulnerable kids. They first build trust and make them feel loved; then they get closer and closer. Sometimes victims don't even want to say anything of what happened to them because they care so much for their perpetrator. Foster kids are especially vulnerable, as they've been so harmed, they look for any type of affection. According to Voices of the Children, it is estimated about one hundred thousand children are sexually exploited in the US, and about 60 percent of them were part of the foster care system.

Lucy's dad normalized what he did at home, by exposing her to sexual behaviors; and it seemed he was trying to either do it again or have her take back what she had shared about the abuse.

I felt powerless. I had to do something. I had to *ungroom* her, but how? Was the example of a healthy family dynamic enough? Was documenting everything sufficient to keep that monster away from her and stop his visits?

We had to be purposeful in how we showed her an alternative life. Little by little, we started. When I played with her, I would add things like, "You know baby, our job is to keep you safe. Grown-ups keep their babies safe." And I would ask her, "What do parents do?" and she would reply, "Keep their babies safe."

If I saw Steve playing with her, that night I would say, "You know baby, grown-ups play without touching kids' privates. Grown-ups don't ask kids to touch their privates, either."

Some mornings, she would come and try to jump into bed with us, and I would not let her be next to Steve, "Baby, you can't lie next to him. He's a grown-up man."

On Friday pizza-movie nights, she would lie next to me on the couch and try to share my blanket, and I would pause the movie and say, "Everyone needs their own blanket. Let me get you one," because I wanted to prevent a future risk of unwanted hands touching her under a blanket.

At bath time, I would say, "We need to close the door, baby; no boys allowed."

"Can you dry me please, Mamma?" she would ask after she was done.

"No, baby, you need to learn how to dry yourself. You're a big girl now!" My heart ached as I said those words. She wasn't. She was still little.

"Why do you call me baby then? You're silly." And she giggled. She was always so logical. Except when it came to her dad.

At night, when she would ask me to tickle her and then say "stop," I would stop. "Why did you stop, Mamma?"

"Because you said 'stop,' and stop is stop, and no is no."

"But I was joking," she told me once.

"I don't know if you're joking. If you say stop, I have to stop. If someone tells you to stop, you have to stop. Got it?"

"Got it, Mamma. Can you tickle me again, please?"

"Yes, baby, because you asked. But remember no one can tickle you in your privates."

And she would just say, "Okay."

One day, scrolling through one of my social media accounts, I read someone saying you can't tell children no one can touch them, because if it happens, they may feel guilty or ashamed. They may think they allowed it when they were not supposed to let them. They could think it's their fault! And if they love the person who did it, they won't want to tell, since they may not want that person to get in trouble.

Oh my goodness. I was trying my best and I was still doing it wrong! I felt so incompetent.

The day after I heard this, I knew I had to change my tactics. I added, "If someone touches you, remember it's not your fault. Even if the kid says 'yes.' It's never the kid's fault." And I would add later, "If someone tells you it's a secret, they're trying to trick you. So it's okay to tell a grown-up. You can tell a teacher, or you can tell us." And finally, I would say, "If you tell, it's not because we want that person to be in trouble. We want to help them, to teach them they made a mistake, so they won't do that again."

I would always add, "Remember, you're safe here, and I love you."

It was such a difficult balance. I didn't want to trigger her trauma, but I wanted her to know it was supposed to be different. But was she listening? Was I doing it right? Was she learning? I needed to teach her so she could be safe even if I wasn't there to protect her. I was just hoping some of it would stick.

A few more months went by, and the pandemic waves made it difficult to have in-person visits with the dad, so we switched to weekly video call visits instead. Lucy couldn't sit still so those were mostly cut short.

It was on one virtual visit I realized what we were doing was working because I heard her say, "Daddy, this is all your fault! If you hadn't made me do that to your privates, we wouldn't be in this mess. This is all your fault Daddy, and you haven't even said sorry."

Ungroom by CarmenMaria Navarro
verb
ungroomed; un**grooming**; un**grooms**
Definition of un*groom, transitive verb*
1. It's the act of teaching what a healthy relationship between adults and kids looks like.
2. When a loving foster parent teaches a child in their care that a pedophile's sexual act or behavior is never the child's fault. *Example: Lucy was being ungroomed by her foster family so she could recognize that what her dad did to her wasn't her fault.*

CHAPTER 17

THE SYSTEM

If you or anyone you know is a victim of domestic abuse, please call 1800.799.SAFE (7233), text START to 88788 or visit https://www.thehotline.org/

"So *every* Monday is 'let's confront your abuser and tell me everything that happened *again*' type of therapy?" Steve sarcastically asked Emily, Lucy's social worker.

He was referring to the Monday visits with Lucy's dad, described as "individual therapeutic sessions." We had gone back to in-person supervised meetings with Lucy, her dad, and a trained clinician, in which they were supposed to work through the sexual abuse and heal. It was followed by a group session of kids her age, with a different therapist.

"It's court ordered," Emily responded, avoiding looking at us.

What the fuck is wrong with the system? With the judge? Why is that pedophile not in jail? Why does she have to go to therapy with him?

I firmly believe therapy is essential in the healing process after experiencing trauma. What I don't understand—and I don't think I ever will—is why these kids must go to sessions confronting their abusers? Was the dad supposed to apologize to complete his program for reunification? But if he did, if in fact he gave her an apology, he would be confessing on record. Maybe it was set out that way, so he would not technically complete the program required by the judge. If he did, could he go to jail? If he didn't, would reunification be over? I don't know. It seemed to be a catch twenty-two. This was so messed up. The only thing I cared about was Lucy and her being triggered after every visit.

When Lucy first joined our home, all these visits were a logistical nightmare. We expected that. What I wasn't emotionally prepared for was to take her to group therapy for sexually abused kids who were so little. No one mentioned why Lucy was in group therapy to begin with. Her intake form didn't say anything about sexual abuse. No one had really told us why she was removed from her home. It was a learn-as-you-go type of deal. And we realized in those sessions, kids sometimes go with their families, even with their abusers.

When we decided to foster, Steve and I had an intense debate on what ages we thought were appropriate for our family to protect our biological kids. We knew children who had experienced or witnessed sexual abuse may demonstrate sexual behaviors beyond what's an age-appropriate exploration of their own sexuality. We had agreed we would take kids who had been sexualized but didn't express sexual behaviors and were younger than our kids. Once our kids were older, we could welcome children with additional challenges. We accepted ages younger than Gema, assuming they would be physically smaller. We limited teenagers. Age and prior exposure are always a risk, so I recommend every foster parent carefully consider the background if they have permanent children at home.

I don't understand why there is so little disclosure. Is it because they believe it could decrease the child's possibilities of finding a home? I agree with maintaining confidentiality, but up to a point. In this case, if I had known (and I know Emily knew Lucy's background), I would have prepared differently. Trying to do what's right for the foster child is great, but what about the other children in the home? Shouldn't the system also be concerned about them?

Before Lucy shared "her story" during our makeup session, I wondered why she had so many issues the days right after each visit. At that time, I didn't understand why a simple ask, like "please lower the TV volume," would escalate so quickly.

And after sharing it, it was as if a dam had been opened and all the water in it gushed out at full speed. She shared and shared and shared. For me, this was awfully hard. It was emotionally devastating to learn more details. I didn't recognize I was experiencing trauma too. I should have been in therapy just to process what I heard.

But sometimes it was unavoidable. She would start talking in the middle of a car ride on a family trip! In front of my biological kids! We had to constantly redirect. Family dinners had to be interrupted, and I would take her upstairs and create space in my room for her to share privately with me. Sunday makeup sessions became "story time."

I would learn the details about the night when she was removed from her house. *I came home from school one day, and Mommy was crying. Auntie had her head on the fridge's door, crying too. I got scared and sat on Grandma's lap. The police came and I got scared, so I started drawing on my little notebook, being a good girl. I was quiet. But the police saw me anyway, and they took me and Bubba and Sissy away.* She described it as going to someone's house, then they kicked her out, and she had to go to someone else's house and someone else's and someone else's until she came to us. And she couldn't live with her mommy or daddy anymore.

Every week, mostly on Monday mornings, Steve sent an email to the full team of social workers and therapists, sharing the positives and the negatives of the week, detailing the post-visit behaviors. It was our way to get on the same page with the therapists, so they could work with her on the most recent issues. Most importantly, it was our way to advocate for her, to document how devastating the effects of the relationship with her dad were. We hoped the consistent patterns would become proof in court. Meanwhile, no lawyer ever showed up. At all.

Over the next few months, we documented, reported, and ungroomed, then documented and reported even more. But we questioned, *How many more details did they need?* What five or six-year-old would invent these graphic descriptions? Actually, what four-year-old would say things like that? Because she was removed from her house at age four. And according to what her mom told me one visit, the abuse must have happened when she was three and her little sister one. So where was her mom? Was she the one who called the police? Was she a victim herself? It's documented that 75 percent of the deaths of women victims of domestic abuse occur when they're trying to leave, and the abuser gets custody of the kids 50 percent of the time (Center for Relationship Abuse Awareness, 2022). I would never know.

Emily constantly told us the goal for Lucy and her siblings was reunification, but how could this be possible in the case of the father? It had been months, and things weren't changing. Despite how much reporting we did, Lucy still saw her mom and her two siblings on Fridays and her dad on Mondays right before the group therapy. Her behaviors escalated after each visit, lasting for a couple of days. The repercussions of her dad's visit would last until Wednesday, and Friday's visit with Mom started a cycle of misbehaving for the full weekend. Thursday had become our only "good" day, where it seemed to be a bit calmer. Our best nights together were on Thursdays and on Sundays after makeup sessions, but for the most part, she demanded more and more attention.

She also increased her aggression toward Gema. We reached the point Gema slept in our bed, while it took hours for Lucy to go to sleep. Gema had basically lost her room. Steve and I had to divide ourselves constantly. One was with Lucy, the other one with Gema, and Iago was left on his own. We had become two single parents trying to manage two separate families.

We asked for more therapy including sessions for Gema and Lucy together, but it took a minute to get Lucy set up—I think in part because we made the mistake of trying to weather the storm, hoping it would get better with time, denying our family was disintegrating. In part, too, it was because we had to justify the higher need for services, and if the county agreed, it would cost them more, including a higher reimbursement to the foster parents. I didn't know this. According to our placement documentation as of November 2021, our county, located in California, pays $1,037 for the basic rate, and it increases up to $2,706 for the highest rate (Intensive Services Foster Care or ISFC). Every state is different, but generally, the state tries to keep those expenses to the lower end.

I wonder how many foster parents increased their complaints so they could trick the system and get the highest possible allowance. Perhaps that's what the county workers are concerned about. Who audits that the money goes to care for the child? In our case, we work through an agency that visits our home and inspects frequently, and we also save and turn in receipts.

Lucy needed the services, though, and so did our whole family. Unfortunately, we didn't recognize how bad things were. Gema was struggling beyond the lack of bonding. The relationship between her and Lucy was corrosive. Gema became increasingly anxious. She developed a skin rash and had nightmares even when sleeping next to me.

Our agency team started to notice it was rough and gave us extra foster parent training. We watched hours of videos of Trust-Based Relationship Intervention training (Karyn Purvis Institute of Child Development, 2022). Shonna also checked in with Gema, but Gema was not sharing much. I searched online for tips or courses; I couldn't find anything. At least nothing specifically designed for the bio kids.

Every month, we had to rate Lucy's behaviors in different categories on a scale from one to ten, one being lacking and ten being excellent. Even the two clinicians who came twice a week to our home to see her weren't enough. Emily kept listening to the calls and one time she said, "I think you should rate her lower than a five in that area." It turns out the number determined the need for services and the rate.

It took almost six months to raise her to the highest level of care, mostly because Emily pushed us to give a low number and I so wished she would have been more straightforward. We should have rated her a one in multiple categories, but we were being lenient, wanting to see improvements. And she *had* improved, but she also became a lot more than we could handle.

It's evident why between 30 to 50 percent of foster parents quit in the first year due to lack of support (Williams-Mbengue, 2019). Wouldn't it be better if Lucy would have come to our home with a support "package" from the get-go? If our family was properly trained including our own children, proactively? If we would've gotten counseling as soon as we asked, for the full family? Including grief counseling when the children leave so we could heal faster and get ready for the next child? Wouldn't that be better in the long-term?

I think unconsciously, we didn't want to see what was in front of us and the damage it was causing to our own child.

I was blind.

But the "system"... the system knows better. It has seen enough, and foster families shouldn't have to learn the hard way, as we did. We learned when it was too late.

CHAPTER 18

BREAKING POINT

FIVE AND A HALF MONTHS

I heard screams. It was Gema. Almost immediately I heard Steve yelling, "Stop!"

I didn't understand what could have caused that commotion. I had asked to be left alone for half an hour since I needed a break. Lucy's need for constant attention was taking a toll on me as well. Steve and I separated the girls every day, but it was becoming increasingly difficult, and we were both exhausted. Recently, we had decided one of us would take time alone while the other supervised both.

The situation had become unsustainable, but we were holding steady knowing it would be over soon. Lucy was meant to go back with her mom in just a few weeks. Her mom had already pushed this by fifteen days, but it was looking good. Her little sister had already been reunified and Lucy and her brother were next. Lucy's mom had shared with me she had split with the dad, and although he was still having weekly visits, there was no talk of reunification with him.

Before I could get out of the bed, Gema came stomping into my room, shaking, lips trembling, tears rolling down her eyes, and a red face.

"She choked me, Mommy! She choked me!" she yelled, shaking her head. I could sense the desperation in her voice. And she added, "I want to die."

I was in shock, wishing this moment could be simply erased, but it wasn't possible.

Lucy was having more and more issues with Gema, but I hadn't seen this level of aggression. Recently, there were a lot of "accidents." She did a cartwheel and "accidentally" hit Gema's arm. Or she dropped a toy "accidentally" on Gema's foot. And each time, she said sorry. At first, we were accepting the "sorrys" at face value, but once we saw the pattern, we decided to be stricter. We instituted the make-up policy, in which the "offender" kid would have to do something nice for the affected one, like make their bed or pick up dishes at dinner or even pay a dollar for broken items. We were hoping to teach consequences while discouraging the behavior. Unfortunately, nothing reduced the number of "accidents." Gema no longer slept the full night, and the stress rash on her hands was very painful.

I hugged Gema intensely. There was not much I could say.

Gema didn't like being around Lucy anymore and had been avoiding her as much as possible, so it was unlikely she would initiate the fight. I wasn't discarding the possibility of Gema being responsible for starting it, but her body language and the way she ranted in frustration, the way her tears rolled down her cheeks with indignation, indicated to me the incident had been unprovoked.

The fight started when Lucy blocked Gema's view of the TV. Gema was sitting on her bean bag trying to play video games and had extended her arm so Lucy wouldn't get any closer. But her hand had touched Lucy, and Lucy's tolerance was low that day. That gesture triggered Lucy and she went ballistic, yelling "Don't touch me!" and jumped on top of Gema and choked her. Steve, who was next to them, had to pull Lucy away from Gema.

My sense of powerlessness overwhelmed me as Gema shared the details. I was devastated by Gema's fear, frustration, and anger toward someone I deeply loved, especially knowing Lucy didn't intend to do this, and once she calmed down, she would regret it. None of this was Lucy or Gema's fault. But for Gema, there was nothing else to give. She sobbed uncontrollably, saying how unfair this was for her; how she would never hit Lucy; that she tried and tried, but Lucy always antagonized her, and now she had attacked her; how she had lost everything: her space, her time with us, her peace.

She had reached her breaking point.

We couldn't continue to put her through this. When we started fostering, Steve and I swore we were always going to put our kids first. We're talking about a six-year-old physically overpowering an eight-year-old. Something I never imagined could happen.

I stayed with Gema the rest of the day. Lucy kept coming out of her room to apologize, and my heart cracked a little every time she tried to talk to Gema. But Gema was done and ignored Lucy, which made Lucy more anxious. It was agonizing.

At night, we switched. Steve stayed in our room with Gema while I did the bedtime routine with Lucy and put her to bed.

"I made a mistake, Mamma. I didn't mean to. I said sorry. Are you 'banning' me because I was bad? Are you sending me away? If you send me away, can you send me back to my mommy?"

My soul crushed. She had referred to the prior house as "banning" her and "kicking her out."

"That's not how it works, baby. The judge is the one who decides when you go to your mommy, and she's working very hard to get you back." But at that point, I knew if her mom delayed reunification once more, we wouldn't be able to keep her past the end of the month, a few weeks from that day. I couldn't bring myself to tell her anything else. Deep down I knew the decision was made the second I saw Gema that afternoon.

I sent an email explaining what happened and called Shonna the next day.

"It seems her bio mom may ask for a few more weeks, maybe a month more," she explained.

"No, please," I begged, as if Shonna had the power to change the circumstances. I started ranting. "Gema can't deal with this anymore. She's now seeing a counselor because of her anxiety. It wasn't this way before. We already separated them and rearranged rooms. I just hope her mom doesn't delay anymore. This is so hard. I can't bear to send her away to strangers if the mom can't take her. Lucy is my baby too. You know I love her. She's thinking she's going back home. I can't do this to her."

As part of Lucy's transition, I had started supervising visits at the park with her mom and her little sister, and every time she asked when she could go back home, I responded, "Your mom is working very hard to get you back, but the judge will decide." Her mom even told her, "I hope soon."

Why was her mom delaying? How could I send her away somewhere else if her mom couldn't take her back? Despite her disruptive behaviors, I had fully fallen in love with this little person.

But I was failing.

I didn't realize in the process of healing Lucy, I was hurting my own child. I didn't recognize the mental health issues my own child had developed, the signs of anxiety and trauma I had been trained to recognize in others. We had taken Gema to the doctor, and she told us her rashes were just allergies, when in fact, it was stress. I wasn't linking it to the other symptoms: lack of sleep, irritability, a new fear of darkness, and separation anxiety. I was so preoccupied with making sure Lucy was safe I had created an emotionally unsafe place for my own baby. Would it have been different if I knew what secondary trauma was and how it could affect us?

It turns out secondary trauma, the duress that happens when someone witnesses or hears firsthand the traumatic experiences of another, has been analyzed and documented. The National Child Traumatic Stress Network explains how secondary trauma affects social workers and others working directly with traumatized children. How could the system miss this for all foster families, and it's not included in our training? Why is everyone in my family not receiving counseling as an essential service?

Gema was beyond secondary trauma, and this last incident brought it to full light. Her heart was being decimated. How didn't I protect her?

~

I recently chatted with a very thoughtful sixteen-year-old, the older brother of Iago's baseball teammate, whose family had unofficially fostered a family member. I wanted to understand what I missed with Gema. He knew of our situation and was kind enough to share his perspective.

"Danzik, you also had a similar experience, didn't you? With a little one who needed a lot of attention?" I asked him.

"Yes," he replied hesitantly. "I didn't have a lot to say because it was my mom's idea. I'm sure a lot of kids feel this way. Maybe yours feel the same. I felt like my voice would go in and right through my parents' ears. You know what I mean? We're just kids. I know I'm not a child, but I'm still a kid, so my opinion just doesn't hold much weight."

He paused for a second and took a deep breath as if he needed the courage to share.

"The family relationships became very difficult because she was really loved. But we'd be sitting down and she'd make a scene, throw a tantrum for no reason. And you can only deal with it for so long before it starts to impact you; all of a sudden, you're grouchy all the time. She broke a lot of family dynamics, and we could do nothing about it. During this time, trying to be with both my parents was impossible. It was hard to spend time with just my mom, so it ended up being me with my dad and my brothers. We all had to accept it; we didn't have a choice. It was pretty draining, and a lot of stuff happened that got me really scared and nervous—just very shaky. It was like a constant threat, looming in the back of our minds, and I'd be like *How long is this going to last before my family breaks?*"

"I'm so sorry. I can't even imagine," I said. Was that how Gema felt, not being able to share? Did Iago feel that way too?

"How was your mom doing with all of this? She must have been so conflicted," I said, thinking about my own experience.

"Oh, she was definitely conflicted. I mean, it's just such a tough situation, and the problem is there's no way to come out on top. There's no way to beat it. It's like there's no win-win; it's a win-lose no matter what. It was a very cinematic thing when it was all happening, like a character being tormented in an old classic. It was either the kid or our happiness as a family, and that was it. No other options. And I'm just a child, and seeing my mom being so upset..." He couldn't finish the sentence.

It hurt to hear him, imagining that's how my own kids felt. "I understand," I replied.

He nodded, maybe because few people understand how fostering impacts your family life.

"I think Gema was bottling her feelings. I know she's much younger than you, and I wonder if she would ever say something to me. Did you ever tell your parents how you felt, or would you share in the future?"

He took a few seconds to respond... almost as if he was debating his answer. "I would never say. There was really no way to speak my mind without feeling incredibly guilty. Because you can't tell somebody. 'I don't want this kid in my life.' A kid who had been abused. I would feel *very* guilty. I think everyone in my family thought we either adopt her permanently or we wouldn't see her again. And those are terrible options. It felt like her life was more important than me being upset about the drama in our family. I couldn't kill the opportunity of somebody who's been abused, to come live with us and have a better life. That's just not right. So no. I really don't think I would share my opinions."

~

Shonna lately said to me, "People don't really think about their bio kids (or other permanent kids in the house); they think the kids will just go with the flow, that they are resilient. But they have feelings too. It's a big thing for them, especially if they're sharing a room. Maybe they shouldn't share a room. They're basically sharing their space with complete strangers, and you expect them to do this willingly, so I always ask how *your* kids are doing. You need to ask your kids as well."

When bio kids would tell Shonna their feelings, she would ask, "Have you told your mom?" and their usual response is, "No, I didn't tell my mom; they really want to do this." So she would remind them, "No, no, you need to tell your mom and dad how you're feeling because we can work on that." But she also says most times the biological kids don't want to seem selfish, impeding on their parents' desires to do something good for the world. "We need to create a space for them to share, though."

I think that's what Gema went through. She wouldn't say how she was truly feeling. She was hiding it. I didn't see it or didn't want to see it, and Shonna didn't notice it either or she would have taken immediate action. Regardless, I didn't create the space for Gema to share. She was holding it all in, and her body couldn't take it, and it was unfair. It's unfair for our permanent kids to take the responsibility of the adults. We can't expect children to handle this without deeper support.

They are kids, and they're sacrificing themselves, deeply suppressing their fears or concerns, so they can help others. Kids like Danzik, like mine, like many other permanent children are unique, generous, and altruistic. We need to shield them. It's not sustainable that we support the kids who come into our care without protecting and caring for our own, including bio, step, adoptive, or long-term placements. It doesn't make sense that this is not seen as an ecosystem, where the health of the foster care system is dependent on the health of the foster families as a whole. We need to look at it holistically, or we will break our own kids unintentionally.

CHAPTER 19

ANGUISH

"I have news about Lucy's mother. Do you have a minute to chat?" Shonna texted a couple of days after the incident between Lucy and Gema.

I didn't, but I replied yes. Lucy's reunification date with her bio mom was fast approaching, and I was anxious the date could change. Things at home were very tense, and we could barely handle it. By then, Shonna should've talked with Emily.

The phone vibrated, and I picked it up instantly. "Hi, Shonna."

"Hi CarmenMaria, thank you for making time. I just hung up the phone with Emily, and there was a development."

I stayed silent, holding my breath. She waited for one second, and she continued.

"There was an incident with Lucy's sister at the ER. They're going to stop providing services to her mom."

I wanted to ask, "What do you mean by 'ER' and 'stop providing services?'" but I feared the answer. *Breathe, just wait, breathe...*

She continued, "The details of the ER visit are confidential, but it must have been pretty bad because they moved immediately to terminate parental rights for all kids. They're all going to be up for adoption. Lucy's sister has already been placed in a concurrent home. Her brother will stay with his current foster family, who wants to adopt him. Emily wants to know if you guys would be willing to keep Lucy as a concurrent placement and adopt her."

My heart raced. I wanted to throw up. I knew the answer. I tried to open my mouth, and no sound came out. I couldn't say it out loud. I stayed silent.

"I know you love her, and you have done your best. You have given her stability and love." She was giving me an out. But there was no "out" for what I was feeling.

I started sobbing. "What happened? What happened to her mom? She was doing so well. I just saw her. What happened? It can't be. I *just* saw her!"

Even if Shonna knew, she couldn't share. I was furious. Why did Lucy have to suffer more? Why did I have to be in the position of this dreaded decision? It wasn't supposed to be this way. I had seen Lucy's mom the prior weekend, and she had come prepared with water, healthy juices, fruit, and snacks. She was doing so well. At this point, we had moved to longer visits at the park, supervised by just Steve or me. I had started to bond with her too; I could see she was making true efforts to her kids back. She had not seen the dad in months, and she had gotten help—therapy and parenting classes. She had found a job, working some nights and some days, so she could be flexible with all the appointments required for her and the kids. Her sister had moved in with her to help with the children while she was working. On every visit to the park, you could see she really loved her kids. She confided in me how hard all of this had been for her as well, that she didn't know the abuse was happening, and she was trying so hard to get her babies back. I rooted for her.

She was also going to let me see Lucy once she went back to live with her. We were going to be in touch. I would babysit. Lucy would have the two of us. One Mommy, one Mamma. I wouldn't need to choose between her and Gema.

WHY DOES IT HAVE TO BE THIS WAY?

The stages of grief took over. Denial. Anger. Bargaining. Depression. Acceptance (Kübler-Ross and Kessler, 2021).

"I want to keep her, Shonna. I want to keep her forever. I can't send her away. Maybe we can... maybe things have calmed down enough between Gema and her, or maybe they can have therapy together. We've been asking for it. Maybe if they go to counseling, they can get along and, in the future, become sisters? Where will she go if she doesn't stay here? She will be devastated, and I will die. I can't let her go. Why couldn't her bio mom keep it together! We can keep her. I want to keep her. She's my baby. She calls me 'Mamma.' I can't do this to her."

I will not accept it. I couldn't. She is my baby!

Denial.

"I know it's really hard for you. Lucy has a lot of potential, and she has been doing great in your home, but it's too much. It's just too much for your family. And I know you could keep trying. You can keep giving, but Gema can't anymore. You know this. Now it's time to draw the line. It is where it's at; it's tough," said Shonna. I knew if I didn't make the decision, she would make it for me.

I paced in my bedroom. My heart was crumbling, and it was coming out of me through my skin. I was shaking.

"I've had other placements in the past, where the foster child's behavior is just so extreme it impacts the bio kids on a deeper level that no one could have ever imagined. It's hard to predict because you've never been in that situation. The first placements are always tough because you don't know how your kids are going to respond until then. I know it's really hard. I know you love her. You have done everything you could. But you know what you need to do," explained Shonna, the voice of reason, an advocate for Gema and us, foster families.

"I don't know how I can let her go. I don't know... I don't know. She's my daughter too."

"If you want to talk with Steve and give me a call later, we can do that. I'll be here but we need to decide soon."

We hung up, not knowing exactly when I would give her the answer we both knew was coming. *I need to figure it out. We have to make it work. Maybe with more time.*

I texted Steve: *Mom screwed up; something happened. All kids are up for adoption.*

At that second, I lacked all compassion for the mom. I despised the dad for what he did to her and the system for not putting him in jail and letting him roam free. Her mom for not figuring it out. I was infuriated at the world. None of this was Lucy's fault. None of it! And here we were.

Anger.

That night, after putting Lucy and Gema to bed, there was more denial, sadness, anger, and bargaining, especially with Steve. He went into protective mode, reminding me of our agreement to always put our kids first—an agreement I had insisted both of us swear on.

I begged him, "Please... Maybe if we bring Lucy's little sister, things may get better. Then she'll have someone she knows and loves and will behave better. Who's going to take care of the little sister?"

"You're forgetting they had to separate them because Lucy was aggressive with her. Lucy had to leave the prior home because she attacked the nine-year-old. You're forgetting we have a child we *have* to protect. She needs us. And she is *ours!*" He raised his voice. His face was red, and his left eye twitched.

"Lucy is my daughter too! Maybe she's not *your* daughter, but she's *my* daughter!" I shouted. I wanted to hurt him as if he were my enemy, as if he were the cause of all the bad in the world. I wanted to hurt someone.

I took a sleeping pill that night. *She's my baby* was my last thought before I fell asleep with my heart torn into a million pieces.

When I woke up the next morning at 6:20 a.m., my eyes were puffy, and my neck was stiff. I had slept wrong, so my right shoulder was hurting too. I turned around to where Steve sleeps, and he was looking at the ceiling, silently.

"Maybe we can keep her," he pleaded. "Remember why we started doing this?"

I nodded.

"We want to keep children safe. We want to give them love. We wouldn't be doing our jobs if we sent her away. We would be failing. We would be giving up. What kind of humans would we be if we gave up on her and let her go? We are her family. We don't give up. Our job isn't done. We fight!" he yelled.

Bargaining.

But the numbing pain also brought clarity. "We need to protect our own kids. Our kids need to feel safe and loved first. If we can't do that, we can't keep fostering. And we both know our own baby is not doing well. We don't want to see it. But she's screaming for help, and we're not accepting it. We need to call Shonna and tell her we decided. It's a horrible decision, but it's the right one," I stated.

We hugged. Tightly. So much that it hurt. I cried, gasping for air. He held back tears, but his body shook. He loved her. She was his daughter too.

"How are we going to tell her?" I asked and before he could answer, I ran to the bathroom to throw up.

Depression? Acceptance?

No.

Anguish

noun

an·guish | \ ˈaŋ-gwish \: extreme pain, distress, or anxiety (*Merriam-Webster Online Dictionary*)

CHAPTER 20

LIFEBOOK

———

"We have to let her go," I told Shonna. It took all human strength to make that phone call.

"Could you please explain to Emily why we can't keep her?" I tried to keep it together, but I couldn't, "We love her. I love her. This is awful. I don't know how we are going to tell her. I'm going to die. I need help." My voice trembled.

"I know you love her. Sometimes these decisions are hard. But you and Steve are doing the right thing. If you decided to keep her, it would have been harder, and at some point, I would have made the call for you. I will do the paperwork for the fourteen-day notice and will give Emily the heads up, so she knows before the next Child Family Team meeting this Friday. We will figure it out. We can do it together. We need to advocate for Lucy and share she needs a home with no children. She needs parents fully dedicated to her. It'll be okay, CarmenMaria. It will hurt, but it will be okay. Gema will be thankful, and she will know you guys protected her."

"Please tell Emily if it takes more than fourteen days to find the right home, we can keep her longer. We just need to find the right family for her. We can't just send her anywhere."

In California, it's required to give at least fourteen days written notice when the child needs to leave your home so the county can review the request and find a suitable family (Advokids, 2022). The issue is time. The older the kids are, the more homes they've been in, or the higher the requirements (such as asking for a home with no other children), the harder it is to place that child. This is why I hate the fact the system is not designed to share all the information related to the child's background. We're not set up for success. No one is. Foster parents can't make an informed decision as to what's best for their own families. If it turns out it's not the right placement, there is another transition and more trauma for both the child and the foster family. If we're good enough to take care of these children, we should be good enough to know what happened to them, so we can make a thoughtful decision.

And what about the support needed? Wouldn't it be nice if the foster family and the foster child could have a full support suite of services? If the system had things figured out, neither foster families nor foster kids would be in this situation.

If I had to let her go, at the minimum, we had to ensure the next home knew, was fully informed, and Lucy went with all the services so we could improve her probabilities of permanency and avoid another traumatic transition.

"Tell her we will keep her for as long as they need to find the right home," I repeated.

~

The days between that phone call and the Child Family Team meeting are blurry. Lucy's routines hadn't changed. She was as loving and as sweet as ever. Every night I said, "I love you, baby," and she would reply, "I love you to the moon and back,

Mamma." The choking incident with Gema seemed to have been a wake-up call for her, since she had never behaved so well. If this had been the child we had the whole time, the end of this story would be different. But it wasn't. As much as we knew it was not her fault, we also knew deep down her remorseful behavior was only temporary.

I wondered if she sensed what was about to happen, if she felt my grief, and if she was doing everything in her power to change the outcome. This made things even worse because it gave us the illusion we could handle it, and this possibility started to corrode my soul. I was going back and forth on what to do. It was torture.

The Child Family Team meeting was around the corner, and I kept having second thoughts. If we were to give Lucy a chance, I had to talk with Gema and determine if she could have a change of heart. It was a long shot, but I was desperate. If we were to be Lucy's forever family, I had to know Gema would be alright. But how could I ask Gema without putting this huge responsibility on her? She was only eight. It was so unfair, but was it worth trying? This was killing me.

The night before the meeting, I decided to delicately feel what Gema was thinking, without telling Steve. "*Amor*, I know Daddy told you Lucy's not going to go back to be with her mommy and she can be adopted."

"Yes, it's so sad. It's going to break her heart because she thinks she's going to go to her mommy," she replied, incredibly empathetically.

"Yes, it's very sad." I paused. *God give me the right words,* "If we were able to keep her and adopt her, now she's behaving better, do you think that would be a good idea?"

She covered herself with the blanket and started crying. "I'm sorry, *Mami*, I'm sorry. I'm sorry."

Oh no! What have I done?

I had broken her! I hadn't protected her again. It was too much for her. Too much for me. How could I have done this to my baby again?

I tried to take it back. "It's okay, *mi amor*, I was just asking to see what you felt. We don't decide where she goes. The judge decides. The judge gets all the reports, so even if we wanted to keep her, we couldn't. The judge already told Shonna Lucy needs a home with no other kids. I was just curious, but nothing we say will change the judge's mind. They already told Shonna Lucy's leaving."

But it was too late. I could see her struggle. I had already hurt her. Again.

The next day I took the day off from work. Everyone was in the video call: the moderators, Lucy's two clinicians, the therapists who saw her at the center for sexually abused victims, Emily, Shonna… and *her mom*. She was looking down, so I couldn't see her eyes or expression. But I could feel her shame. It resembled mine. The guilt consumed me, and I was shaking, dreading the moment it was my turn to talk. I became angry at her, blaming her for the situation.

As the moderator started naming who was in the call, Shonna texted me, "I gave Emily the heads up. She is going to ask you. Keep it brief and focus on what she needs in the next home."

Instead of going around the room with the usual status updates, Emily interrupted the moderator and said: "I understand CarmenMaria and Steve are giving their fourteen-day notice."

The virtual room went quiet. Everyone was on mute, but the silence was piercing my already-broken heart and making it unbearable to breathe. Then I saw Lucy's mom. It became evident she was the only one who didn't know. She looked up, coming closer to the camera, tears started rolling down her eyes. She un-muted, then muted, then un-muted, as if she was about to speak, but muted again. She lowered her head and started crying.

And my unwavering rage toward her dissolved instantly. I saw her raw pain. Her helplessness. And although I was grieving, I wanted to reach through the monitor and hug her. We were both losing our baby.

"CarmenMaria or Steve, is there anything we could do to save the placement?" the moderator asked.

There was a lot that could have been done.

Steve held my hand, and we looked at each other. The image of Gema crying the night before, covering herself under the blanket, full of guilt, came to mind.

And with a strength I didn't know I had, I said, "Unfortunately, no. There is nothing we can do at this time. We love Lucy, and we wish it was different. But our bio child is in distress, and it's been going on for months. Her well-being is at risk, so unfortunately there is nothing we can do. I'm so..." by the end of that sentence, I couldn't get the final words out. I put my head on Steve's chest and started sobbing. He muted us.

Shonna jumped in. She explained Lucy's physical aggression toward our daughter and advocated for new requirements in her next home. She talked about the highest levels of care... somewhere in there, I said we could keep her until they found the right home. Steve nodded. The moderator set up a time to meet the following Tuesday for an update on finding a new placement. We agreed no one was going to say anything to Lucy until things were fully settled.

On Tuesday Shonna texted me, "They canceled the meeting today. They found a home. Lucy will leave early Thursday."

This Thursday? It can't be. I was in complete shock, and I texted Shonna without waiting for answers, "So soon? I won't have time to pack all her things. Is there a transition plan? Can you ask if it could be at 3 p.m.? Could you please ask if they can come and pick her up here, so it feels more comfortable? I don't want to drop her off at the crisis center and transfer her in the parking lot like when she came over."

Shonna texted back the family taking Lucy wasn't concurrent—they didn't intend to adopt—but was an ISFC (Intensive Services Foster Care) home, which is the highest level of home care available. They had arranged daily visits from her clinicians, and she was also going to be seen by a psychiatrist.

I knew she was going to receive more services because we advocated for her, but why did it take so long? Why did it take four homes of unresolved issues, four homes in which she could have gotten the help she needed? Where would she be if we had all received services earlier? Would the outcome have been different?

It would be six transitions if she got adopted after this home. Each transition was a loss, another trauma, deepening the sense of abandonment, decreasing the chances for healthy attachments (Advokids, 2022). I witness firsthand how these children have low self-esteem and believe they're not loved or deserving of love. This "side effect" doesn't affect the foster children exclusively. I chatted with one foster parent who shared his biological children suffered from grief once their foster siblings left, and they weren't allowed to see them. They were also reluctant to build a relationship with their new foster siblings, fearful it would hurt when they left.

Shonna let me know we would have a conference call on Thursday, including the new foster parents, and that's when we would give the news to Lucy, so she wouldn't have time to think about it. Neither one of us agreed. Shonna had proposed to Emily a transition period, but Emily thought we should just rip the Band-Aid off, and that's what we had to do.

I had no voice anymore. I had been Lucy's mom for the last six months, and I had no say.

I called Shonna. I couldn't stop crying. "Will they let me see her again?" I asked.

"There is a chance you may not. We can ask the new foster parents if they will let you visit, but it's unlikely you will see her." Then she said, "Don't forget to do a lifebook."

Yes, a life album. Lifebooks "is a tool to help children (in the system) better understand their past [...]. A lifebook can offer ways of tracking placement histories" (Child Welfare Information Gateway, 2022).

The prior foster parents had sent Lucy with a little black photo album filled with pictures of her prior life. They took the time and care to fill it out. There was not one page left. There was another album of her and her bio family, including numerous pictures of her dad. The pedophile had a lot of sections in her *lifebook*. And Lucy carried it everywhere to remember where she came from.

If I had to let her go, I was going to make sure *our* lifebook was better than any other, with tons of pictures of us hugging, smiles, and kisses, of Christmas and her birthday, our nice makeup sessions, her doing gymnastics, the zoo visit, and the snow trip. A lifebook so she would remember how much we loved her, how much *I* loved her. So she would forget I betrayed her, I preferred my own biological child over her, and I was just like her dad—one more person who betrayed her.

CHAPTER 21

THE LETTER

"I wrote a letter to Lucy's new foster parents. I signed it for both of us," I told Steve the day before Lucy left. "Shonna already read it, and she thought it was okay, nothing confidential to worry about."

"I see. Can I read it?"

"Here." I handed him a copy.

Our names are CarmenMaria and Steve. We have been Lucy's foster parents since last September, and we would like to share a few thoughts in hopes her transition to your home is easier.

To start, we love her deeply. Our intent was always to foster, but when Lucy became open for adoption, we struggled with the decision. Transparently, our eight-year-old bio child has been struggling tremendously. We always told Lucy it's not us deciding; it's the judge. Please help us reinforce that message. She feels she gets kicked out or "banned" from others' homes because she makes mistakes. We always told her our time with her was going to be temporary and we love her. As she goes with you, I would like her to feel she's not being kicked out.

We are hopeful she finds a loving home with you until she gets adopted, and we thought we could share a bit of what we've observed. With love and patience, she's improved so much.

A few of the positives:

- She's a great singer, whistler, and Spdancer. She will dance after every movie's final credits. She enjoys kids' pop and the music from many Disney+ movies. I will put those songs on, and we will sing together, or at night we will play a game of humming and will have to guess each other's songs.
- She's an incredible gymnast. When things open up, it would be great if you could sign her up for gymnastics. Ask her about the flips and the cartwheels.
- She loves to help, but you need to supervise. She helps Steve in the yard, and she helps me cook. She will season the fish, beat the eggs, or roll the dough for handmade pasta. She's great at following instructions. Just beware of things that are hot, especially the stove or oven. She likes to touch everything, and you need to supervise even when she puts bread in the toaster since she will push it so strongly it gets stuck (last time smoke came out of it).
- She's very active, and she's fearless, constantly running, jumping, and climbing. Therefore, she's quite prone to accidents, falling, or bumping into things. Just ask her to slow down a bit. She really loves her scooter and running around. She loves going to the park. Last weekend we went to see snow, and she was very good at sledding. She has never been to the beach;

it's something we were planning to do this summer. She doesn't know how to swim though.

- She's a talented artist. You give her a cardboard box, scissors, and markers and she will make anything. We usually get her temperas and canvases for her to paint or chalk for our patio. Avoid acrylic... We've had terrible accidents with them.
- She likes watching unicorn, little pony, or mermaid shows.
- She likes dolls, playing in the kitchen, and loves dressing up.
- She really likes doing my makeup. We will sit for hours doing this. I usually tell her makeup is only for adults, but occasionally I let her use my pink lipstick. She will share "some things" when she is doing makeup. She refers to them as "my story." Beware of non-washable nail polish; her accuracy is not good when painting nails.
- None of her behaviors at home show up in school. She's doing extraordinarily well there, so much so she didn't need a parent-teacher conference. She's still working on spelling basic words and her numbers, but she has made a lot of friends, and the teacher says with re-direction, she does very well. She has a crush on a little boy. She's very friendly, and her classmates love her.
- She's quite funny and witty. She likes playing Name Five, puzzles (seventy-two pieces), cards, memory. We have a little Foosball table; she's good at that too. Any boardgame. She likes making funny faces and telling jokes, knock-knock, and truth or dare.
- She gets dressed on her own, picks her own clothes, and attempts to wash her hair on her own. She may let you do a half ponytail or half braid. She likes wearing costumes instead of outfits.
- It has taken a few months, but she has become more affectionate with time and much more aware of her feelings and understanding of others' feelings. Sometimes I will say, "I'm really

struggling today. I'm very tired. Could you please help me out?"
And she asks me to do the same with her.

We would also like to share the areas she's still working on (and how far she's come in about six months); as well as some tips in case these behaviors show up:

- When she arrived, she transformed herself into a cheetah or a puppy with frequency. The cheetah scratched us. Later, she was able to verbalize the animals meant she was sad or scared. This has subsided for the most part. When it happens, I ask her calmly if she can be a human since I'm scared of the cheetah. She also has the option of being a nice cheetah who doesn't hurt people, or she can be a cheetah in her room. My bio child gave her a cheetah stuffy so she can channel her feelings through it.
- She doesn't like to be alone at all. At first, we always had to be with her. This improved with time. We repeat she's safe in this house, and we leave a night light and our bedroom door unlocked so she can have access. She will wake up in the morning and come to our room. She's just starting to respect our sleep, and she will quietly play or watch a Disney show.
- Sometimes she will throw impressive tantrums... When she is calm and before a tantrum happens, I would ask her how she would like me to react if she throws one. She told me to say, "Please calm down, and please respect me." I started noticing when a tantrum was about to start, so before it did, I would tell her I could see she was struggling, and I asked how I could help her. I would ask her to breathe as if she was blowing a hot pizza. But sometimes despite our tries, she will still throw a tantrum. It will pass, and she will regret it. If I ground her, I like to stay with her or nearby so she's not alone.

- If she starts snapping at us, we say, "Lucy, you're snapping. Could you please respect us? I'm asking nicely," and she will generally stop.
- She's learning a simple "sorry" is not a pass and poor decisions have consequences. Proportionate to her "offense," we have tried taking privileges away (screen time), time out (six minutes). The highest level of consequence for hitting was missing family movie night once. She asked if that meant she wasn't part of the family, and we responded while she's here, she's a member of the family and that meant following the rules as everyone else and being nice to others.
- She gets very upset if she feels not listened to or if you don't believe her.
- She has been exposed to horror movies. AVOID clowns at all costs.
- Shopping with her is tricky... She tries to grab everything, and it takes forever to get back to the car.
- She's a picky eater (details attached).
- After her parents' visits or her therapy sessions, we will give her a sucker that she chews intensely. After dad visits, we go to McDonald's, which is her comfort food.
- Sometimes she will talk in a lot of detail of what happened to her. I usually say, "I'm sorry. You're very brave. It's not your fault. You are safe here." She's finally realizing it's not her fault.
- Lucy benefits from a clear and consistent routine. Attached is her schedule.

Finally, we would love to stay in touch. She's an extraordinary little girl, we love her deeply, and we would like her to know we're still here for her (we don't want her to feel she's been discarded, kicked out, or banned). We will respect your space but would love to be part of her life.

We always told her when she leaves the house, we would like to stay in touch. In time, maybe we can have her for a sleepover or do respite, playtime in the park or here. We will miss her.

Please reach out whenever you are ready. Our contact information is attached.

With affection,

CarmenMaria and Steve

———

"I think you captured it beautifully," Steve assured.

I hoped the new foster parents didn't think I was being arrogant. My intent was for Lucy to adapt as soon as possible without oversharing.

"I hope they call us, and we see her often." I started crying again.

"I'm sure they will, sweetheart. It'll be okay," he replied.

I was hopeful. But I didn't see her soon... Her new foster parents had different plans.

CHAPTER 22

NOT LIKE THIS, MAMMA

———

It was Wednesday night, and I was agonizing.

Steve and I had decided he would tell the kids Lucy was leaving the next day, as the judge had ordered, they could say goodbye after school, and we would also ask her new foster parents if we could see her soon. She would probably need a few weeks to adapt, but it wasn't going to be our last day seeing her. I didn't really know if this would be true, but I needed to be hopeful. I couldn't deal with more than one heartbreak that day.

While Steve shared this, I put Lucy to bed. The day had gone by like any regular day: She went to school, came back, we played games, had dinner, she showered, I brushed her hair. We laughed, we tickled, we hugged. She wanted to watch a show before going to bed, so I put on her favorite cartoon, and by the time we finished a second episode, she was sound asleep. It was ironic. On her last night, she felt comfortable enough to fall asleep on my lap for the first time.

Thursday came—same people, same time, same video conference. Emily started, "Well, we have good news. We found a home for Lucy; they're willing to take her today. In fact, the new foster parents are in this call already.

CarmenMaria and Steve, they agreed to pick her up at your home at 1 p.m."

The new foster parents were there, but their camera wasn't on. They introduced themselves. Mostly the husband spoke while she stayed quiet. Lucy's mom didn't say a word the whole time; she just kept wiping away her tears. I felt her grief.

Shonna texted, "Remember, they have the highest certification level for kids with extra needs and no kids her age. That's good."

No. It's not good. We can't let her go. It can't be today. I won't even have time to pack her things.

I jumped quickly after their introductions, "Could I ask if instead of one, it be at 3 p.m.? We have a lot of things to pack, and I would like our kids to say goodbye, and they won't be back from school until 2:30 p.m. Maybe we can also tell her we're not disappearing from her life. We could be like extended family. We can always babysit, and we can talk with her whenever you feel is appropriate." It was a lot for them to agree on the spot.

"3 p.m. is fine. That's not a problem, yes," said the husband. *Did he say yes to us staying in her life too?*

The moderator said, "Can we call Lucy to give her the news?" in a tone that made it seem like it was some happy event. It was like she had her to-do list and she needed to go through the motions and check each box as completed. *What about a transition plan? What about spending a few days here and a few days there? What about more time? I need more time.*

"Before we call her, we need to talk about who's telling her and how we are telling her. Emily, we think it would be a good idea you share, and we tell her the judge has decided," instructed Shonna, in a determined tone.

Thank goodness for her. Everyone agreed and Lucy's clinician said he and the other clinician could come to our home right after the call so they could support Lucy through the packing and during the transition.

I was grateful.

"It's time to bring Lucy in," Emily said.

"Let me get her," I muttered.

I wiped off my tears. My body weighed four hundred tons, and I stumbled as I got up. Everything felt like a nightmare, and I waited for Steve to pinch me and say there was another option. But there wasn't. I was barely breathing, and the little air I could get tasted like despair.

"Hey sweetheart, leave the tablet for a second and come with me, please. We're on a video call, and Emily wants to talk with you for a minute."

Lucy walked happily to the room, unaware of what was about to hit her. I gave her my seat, and she took a second to get comfortable, her legs hanging in a relaxed pose. She looked at the screen and immediately saw her mom. "Hi, Mommy!"

"Hi baby," Lucy's mom answered and stopped there. There was no "I miss you," like there always was.

"How are you doing, Lucy?" asked Emily right away.

"I'm good," she replied and stayed quiet after that.

Usually, we brought Lucy at the beginning of these calls, and we kicked off the session by saying all the positives we had observed that month. How much she had improved, how her school was going, how she liked to dance or help me cook, or how she had put her laundry away. I made a point to be very specific. My guess is she was expecting the same process because she was just waiting.

Emily started, "Remember, Lucy, when we talked about the judge, and how the judge was going to have a meeting? Well, the judge had the meeting, and they decided it's better for you to not be in CarmenMaria and Steve's house anymore."

She jumped off the chair, excitedly looking at her mom on the screen. "Am I going back home?"

Her mom looked down.

"No, you have to go to a new home with a new family. We think it's the best for you so you can get more help there," Emily replied.

She stopped. Her smile slowly faded, her face started to get red, and she looked at me while tears poured out of her eyes. She got hold of the blanket near me, lifted her legs, crawled into a fetal position, and hid under it. I tried to hug her. She pushed me away and quickly went under the chair so we couldn't see her.

Emily kept talking. I don't remember much. I could swear she said we were always going to be there for her, this was not a final goodbye, and we could visit.

"*Amor*, sweetheart, I'm sorry. This is not your fault. This is nothing you did," I whispered to her. No one else said anything. Or at least I don't remember anyone. It was just her and I, and the rest of the world didn't exist.

She uncovered her face. "Why can't I go home or stay here? You said you weren't going to 'ban' me. You said you weren't going to kick me out. You said I had to be better. I've been good, Mamma. I've been good! Why can't I go home or stay here?"

I couldn't keep it together, and I started crying.

The laptop was somewhere there, but I wasn't participating anymore. There was silence. Everyone was a witness of this tragedy, including the new foster parents. No one said anything. It was Lucy and I alone talking.

Lucy was right. It was impossible for her to comprehend. Every time she misbehaved, when she would break or throw things at me, yell, insult, or harm me, I would tell her we were not kicking her out. I had said that.

I had lied.

I never imagined I would be in a situation where I had to pick one child over another. I never thought this scenario was even possible. I was kicking her out. I was choosing one daughter over the other, and no words, no therapist would be able to take away the overwhelming guilt, loss, and devastation.

She stood up and ran to her room crying. I ran after her. She hid under her bed, and I joined her. I could barely fit. I hit my head and elbow, but it didn't matter. Nothing mattered.

"*Amor*, I'm sorry. I am really sorry. I love you. I love you. Please come out."

"No. If you love me, why can't I stay here?"

Because I chose Gema over you. Because I'm no better than your dad. Because I'm the worst piece of shit that exists. Because I'm a fucking failure.

"It's not up to us, sweetie. Remember when I said this was your home for now but we're not your forever home and at some point, the judge was going to decide and you will have to leave?" Who was I bullshitting? I knew the truth.

"Yes, Mamma, but not like this. It was not supposed to be like this." She went further back into the corner under the bed, far enough where I couldn't reach her.

CHAPTER 23

DEPARTURE

"Why can't I go with my mommy? Or stay here with you? I will be good, Mamma. I will be better with Gema, I promise," she mumbled from the corner under the bed.

She knew, and it broke me.

We both stayed there for what seemed like years. She got close enough to let me hug her, and we both cried. She kept saying, "I will be good. I will be better with Gema. I promise. Can I stay?"

"*Amor*, this is not your fault. There is nothing you did or could do. I can't keep you. The judge is the one who decides, and we can't control it. But Emily says we can talk with your new foster mother and ask when we can visit." I lied about the judge. It had been me. I didn't want her to think it was her fault, to feel she wasn't loved enough. I didn't want her to hate me.

And, an instant later, she suddenly stopped crying, and she switched to business mode. I think she needed to go through the next phase as fast as possible because she couldn't deal with the heartache either. She came out of her bed and without looking at me anymore, she just started pulling her clothes out of the drawers. She asked where she should put her things, and Steve brought a few suitcases that were supposed to be for when she returned to her mom. She started packing in silence, detached. I tried to help, but she wouldn't let me. It killed me to see this little person, whom I loved infinitely, virtually alone, scared, getting ready to leave.

~

The rest of the day was a blur. I think my mind couldn't fully process it. I remember her repeating over and over, "At what time are they coming? What are their names? Do they have kids? Let's keep packing. I don't need help, Mamma." She went through the motions. I went through the motions.

Her two clinicians came and talked with her. They brought her a McDonald's chicken nugget Happy Meal, cookies, candy, and a new stuffy. Was it a unicorn? I only remember she liked it. They went outside to play, and they talked. She laughed and looked happy, but I knew another piece of her had just died.

At some point, her main clinician Raul came to me and asked, "How are you doing?"

I started sobbing uncontrollably. "Not well. I'm sorry. I don't want her to see me this way."

"It's okay, and it's okay she sees you this way. It's okay for her to know you're sad she's leaving, that you love her."

"I want her to stay, but we can't..." I tried to explain again something he already knew. "I'm sorry."

"I know. You need to know you gave Lucy a family, and that's invaluable."

At that moment, both kids arrived from school. Iago helped Steve move all her luggage downstairs. Gema told her she could take the little toy kitchen set with her. I think she felt guilty too.

We had miscalculated how much stuff she had accumulated while she was with us. We didn't even have enough boxes to pack it all. We emptied a tub of Christmas decorations to put her things in because I wasn't sending my baby away with garbage bags.

Raul, the other clinician, and Lucy came into the living room asking at what time they were coming to pick her up.

"At three, baby," I replied.

"Can they come earlier?" she asked.

I felt my heart being stabbed, but I understood her. "They'll be here soon, *amor.*"

Gema took her upstairs to watch a movie on her tablet. Steve came back with the photos, and I rushed to assemble the lifebook before they picked her up. I wrote on the back of every picture the date, where we were, and our names. I also framed a large photo with a collage of thirty pictures. I wrote "We love you" and "I love you" on multiple pictures, and I wrote my phone number. *I won't ever change this number. I hope you keep the album forever and one day you turn around the picture and call me if you ever forgive me.*

Her new foster parents arrived. They seemed friendly. They brought another little girl, and I immediately thought, *Weren't they supposed to have no other kids?* Almost reading my mind, the foster mother shared her foster girl was returning home to be reunited with her dad that weekend.

Lucy didn't want to come down. She hid in her empty room, under the bed. Gema went upstairs to calm her down. She brought her downstairs, holding hands, and hugged her. I know she didn't want that outcome either.

I gave her foster mom the letter and told her to read it when she had a moment, and I gave Lucy her lifebook and the framed collage. I told her again I loved her, and her new foster family had our number, and I hoped to see her soon. Her foster dad agreed and said we could see her the next weekend or the following weekend. We would talk during the week to coordinate. That comment carried me through the last goodbye.

She got into the car, gave me one last hug and one last "I love you," and she left.

I went upstairs and collapsed. The next few hours and days were unbearable. I kept reminding myself this was best for all of us. Part of me wanted to believe she would get the attention and love she needed to heal in her new home because of everything we did, because we advocated so much for her. I needed to think she was better off with them than with me.

As I closed my eyes lying in bed that evening, I forced myself to remember what Raul, her clinician, said before he left. "I know you're devastated, but please hold on to this: This is the first time Lucy has experienced a family. I've worked with many, *many* kids through the years and a lot of them won't ever experience having been in a family. They may go through their whole childhood, sometimes life, and not know what that is. *She now knows.* What you gave her will stay with her forever."

Forever a family were the last words I had in my mind before dozing off that night.

CHAPTER 24

THE JOB

It had been two and a half months since Lucy had left, and her foster parents wouldn't let me see her or talk with her.

We had taken a break from fostering, and we had been focusing mostly on Gema. She was doing much better, thank goodness. We had gone back to our regular routines and outings. We took a trip, the kids were enjoying golf and baseball, and we were healing as a family. Everyone had seamlessly settled into a calmer life, but I still grieved.

I felt no one understood she was still my baby, and the lack of contact killed me. I feared she would either forget me or resent me because she thought I lied to her, that I didn't truly love her. I had failed her; I betrayed her. I gave her away. Just like her dad betrayed her.

Some days I felt I was dying, that with every breath a piece of my body was becoming putrid, consumed by grief.

I was in agony.

I tortured myself with questions. *What could I have done? Sacrifice my own? Who knows what would have happened with Gema if Lucy stayed?*

How could I love someone who's not mine so much, someone who puts my own child's well-being at risk? No one understood it, and I felt so alone. She was gone, and everyone had just moved on. Everyone kept going on with their lives, but I missed her. I missed every night after dinner, going to the bathroom, and brushing our teeth together. I missed the tickles and the laughs. Every night, I tortured myself while I played the memories of our bedtime routines.

"On the count of three. Go!"

We brushed our teeth.

"Who did it better, Mamma?"

"Me," we'd say in unison. We'd laugh, with toothpaste still dripping.

Of course she always won. She had to.

"Piggyback ride to bed, Mamma?"

"Hop on, baby."

"Mamma, do you remember when we watched Monsters, Inc.*?"*

"Yeah, baby. we just watched it."

"I think Sully and Mike are foster parents. They keep Boo safe."

"Yes, they do. You're so smart. I love you, sweetheart."

"Don't call me sweetheart."

"Okay, Lucy."

"Ooookay, you can call me sweetheart." She would laugh.

"Okay, sweetheart." More laughs. "I love you."

"I love you more, Mamma. I love you to the moon and back. No, I love you to heaven and back."

I loved her to heaven and back too, but she did love me more. Because I was the one who let her go. She would never know it ripped me apart and I was in eternal penance for it.

"Can we play I Spy, Mamma? How about the question game?"

"Okay, but it's bedtime. We can do five more minutes."

"How about six? I turned six, so six."

"That's not how it works. That's for time out, but okay, six."

"Pause! Don't start the six yet. I need to go potty."

"Agaaaain, baby?"

"Maaaamma... you know I go potty just before bedtime... The other potty time is just an extra."

Giggles. Smiles. Hugs. Pause. Toilet flushing.

"Don't forget to wash your hands, sweetie."

"I know Mamma, I know. You don't have to tell me."

"Of course, baby."

"Okay, you can un-pause now."

Twenty minutes would go by. More laughs, more hugs, more games.

"Okay, baby, it's bedtime. Night night. I love you."

"I love you more, Mamma, to heaven and back."

Two and a half months of missing every second of it. She was gone. Fully gone, and they didn't let me see her or talk to her.

I would text her foster mother every other Thursday asking how she was doing. I would get a quick text back saying, "All the same. Visits with her mom and her dad are not as frequent. She's doing well here."

So her dad can see her but I can't? She's doing well here as opposed to what? My house?

Sometimes I would text her, "Do you think I could see her or have a video call at some point?" and in those weeks, I wouldn't get an answer, so I desisted because I didn't want to risk not knowing anything about her.

As time went by, her responses became shorter: "The same. All good here."

I felt like a failure, and I questioned, *How can I do this again? I can't bear this.* I shared this with a friend, and she said, "But you have your own kids. And what did you expect? Wasn't this supposed to happen?"

And this is such an unfortunate misconception. I've heard from so many foster parents how even if the child goes back home and they're happy for them, they still grieve. It's a loss, the same way people lose a child or a loved one. We grieve at different levels, and everyone in the family may have a different pace. Sometimes the loss is deep. And that's what Lucy was for me, and I hate when people minimize the loss because we signed up to do this job.

Isn't this how it's supposed to be? Yes and no. No, because you always want your own story to be different; you hope it will have a good ending. And yes, because you also know it sometimes ends in heartbreak. To make a difference in these children's lives, you're supposed to get in and love them.

IN. DEEP.

You have to go deep so they can have a chance to heal. That's how it works! They need to feel loved so they can feel safe and heal. And little by little, you lower your guard, you feel safe—like those six minutes at bedtime will always be there—and you decide to love them and to feel too. It's a decision.

But it hurts like hell. We know the risks, and we still choose to do it. And to some we are heroes. But how can I be a hero if I failed her? I'm no hero. I should've noticed I needed more help so I could have kept her. I thought we could all weather it. I was arrogant and naive.

Now I felt Gema and my family were in a better place, I needed to start taking time to heal myself, to look for counseling, to go back to my support groups, to take care of me. I needed to get ready for the next one. That was the job. This job is about getting *in*, like an undercover cop, an undercover parent. At some point, you need to come out, regroup, and heal before you get back in.

For the next one, we were going to be more mindful of our own children. And the next one wasn't going to replace Lucy. But if I was lucky, if we did the job right, it would hurt again just as much.

That's the "job." And it's brutal.

CHAPTER 25

ACCEPTANCE

To: Emily
Cc: Shonna
Subject: Lucy

Dear Emily,

Hope this email finds you well.

It's been almost three months since Lucy left our home and since we last talked with her.

In your last email, you asked us to take a step back because Lucy was missing us too much and she was misbehaving. And we have done that. We wanted to give the new foster family space, as well as ensure Lucy has the highest chance for success in her new life.

And now, we respectfully ask you to reconsider us being part of her life in some capacity.

When she left, we told her she was not losing us. She was adding another family. We told her we loved her and she most likely would see us soon. Maybe she could come overnight or to watch a movie, or we could babysit for her new foster family.

I have the profound feeling I am betraying her and somehow the system can be improved. My instinct is saying we shouldn't be another loss for her. She won't understand what happened, but I would like her to know we love her, we didn't lie to her, we are not another person who she trusts and betrays her. We would like her to know she's still loved and missed.

We are not experts, but I would imagine maintaining bonds with people who care for her and are good role models is a good thing. We could be like an extended family. Why can't those bonds be healthy in her development? I would imagine the benefits would outweigh the negatives.

At your next Child Family Team meeting, could you please consider our request? Maybe we can visit her for a bit or meet at a park? Or maybe we can call her?

Thank you in advance,

CarmenMaria

"I wrote Lucy's social worker an email and copied you," I shared with Shonna.

"I know. I saw it. It was well written. Did she get back to you?" she asked.

"Crickets," I replied.

Maybe if I had started my email telling Emily we both are liars and we both lied to Lucy because we told her I wasn't disappearing from her life, maybe if I insulted her, she would have answered.

"I texted the foster mother," I told Shonna.

"Oh, yes? What did she say?"

"Her text this week said her visits with her dad are now once a month and with her mom every other week. She thinks Lucy will be open for adoption soon because her parents' rights are being terminated at the next court hearing. They're waiting to get approval from the judge to medicate her because she's hyper and she's having very disruptive behaviors at school. Her school calls every day... That's new. She was doing well in school here. I know she's active, but I don't think she needs to be medicated. Good news about her dad, though."

I continued, "But she won't let me see her. When I asked when I could see her, she said it's not up to her but to Emily, when I know it's not. Emily last time said it was her foster mom who asked for us to stay away. She also made sure I knew she was doing me a favor by sharing things with me. And I had to swallow my pride and say thank you, because I'm afraid if I say something, I won't ever hear back from her. She did send me a picture of Lucy. She looks healthy."

"At least she's keeping you in the loop," Shonna replied.

"I miss her," I said, bursting into tears.

"I know you do," Shonna reassured me. "I know it's difficult. Sometimes the kids go back to their parents and the parents don't want any contact with the foster family. They want to get past that period in their lives and forget it ever happened. It's hurtful for them too. Sometimes the new foster family needs time to bond or they may feel the child will be impacted negatively if they see the prior foster parent. Other times, the child may feel conflicted as well. It's confusing for them. It varies. We just can't control what will happen. But you had to let her go. It was inevitable; it was not going to end up well for your family. You did your best. Everyone did their best."

Although I was hearing what she was saying, I don't think I was fully processing it. "What could I have done differently to keep her?"

"It's done, CarmenMaria. But if you ask me, you could've separated the girls and put them in different rooms sooner. You would have given your daughter some space. More for Gema than for Lucy. We had talked about it, but we dragged it out for one reason or another. I don't think it would've changed the outcome, though, because Lucy was aggressive to Gema, and she needed *all* your attention. She needed everyone's attention. And you know your daughter wasn't going to fight or beg. That's just not who she is. She's kind; she would've felt guilty. You did the right thing. You wouldn't have been able to keep her; it would have just dragged out a few more months, that's all," she stated.

Her honesty hurt, but it's what I needed to hear. I know we dragged out the room separation. We hoped and waited for those two to get along, but we should've had them in separate rooms to begin with.

"It was a hard decision, but it was the right decision. You have to know you did the right thing. You gave her love, a safe place, a family. Your family will always be her reference point. You will always be in her heart even if she doesn't remember you when she grows up," she affirmed.

I managed to mumble, "I hope she remembers me."

~

I continued to text Lucy's foster mother every other Thursday, sometimes with no response. A few times she said she misbehaved, missed me, and asked about me, so they needed more time before I could be in touch. The rest of the time she just responded, "She's doing fine here. I will let you know if anything changes."

One day I was so desperate for news I messaged Lucy's bio mom through Facebook. She told me sadly they were terminating her parental rights and Lucy was going to be up for adoption by her paternal grandparents in a different state. "I'm not a bad mother, I really tried my hardest."

I believed she tried. I witnessed it in those days at the park. I understood her loss.

One evening, two months later, I got an unexpected text from her foster mother: "We're here at the Crisis Center, and we will have to stay longer. Would you like to come and see her?"

I didn't ask what made her change her mind. I told Steve I had to run to the office. Gema was nearby, and I didn't want to risk her hearing if I told him the truth. I grabbed a juice and cookies and left. I drove as fast as I could, borderline reckless. I wanted to see her so badly.

I arrived at the Crisis Center after they closed. The last time I'd been there was to pick Lucy up. The parking lot was desolated. I didn't park in the cargo area but a few spaces away from a lonely SUV.

I stepped out and turned around as I saw Lucy jumping out of it. I ran. She stood there still.

I slowed down, squatted, and said, "Oh my goodness! You have grown so much! I've missed you! Can I hug you?"

She nodded and threw her arms around me. One arm and one cast, to be precise. They had to stay late as they reported the incident. It happened in school when she fell off the playground. "I had nothing to do with it," the foster mother clarified.

For the next hour or so, we played, we ran, we giggled, we hugged many times. She asked if she could come and stay with us again.

"I wish, *amor*, but you will have to ask your foster mom."

She turned around to her foster mother and said, "Mommy, could I come and stay with her?" She turned around to me. "What was your name again? I'm sorry. I don't remember."

An overwhelming sense of loss grabbed me. It hurt. I knew it was natural. She needed to have a mommy. She needed to heal. But it was still so difficult to hear. Did she remember how much I loved her?

"It's okay, baby. You can call me CarmenMaria, or you can call me Auntie."

Her foster mother said she couldn't go with me and it was time to leave. "Ten more minutes to play, and we need to head home. Dad is waiting."

I swallowed my pain and nodded. "Let's go play for ten minutes, baby."

We ran to the playground and laughed. The tickle lettuce and the tickle tomato came out. We hugged again. Before we said goodbye, she said, "I love you to heaven and back."

"I love you too baby, to the moon and back."

"I love you more, then."

"Why do you say that?"

"Because heaven is farther than the moon, and I love you to *heaven* and back."

That was the last time I saw her. I may not be her mamma anymore, but she remembered my love, and a little part of my heart healed.

Acceptance

noun

ac·cep·tance | \ ik-'sep-tən(t)s , ak- \

Definition of *acceptance*

1. the act of accepting something or someone *acceptance* of responsibility

(*Merriam-Webster Online Dictionary*)

PART III

SHORTCOMINGS

CHAPTER 26

13 Y/O AA F, URGENT

"13 y/o AA F, Urgent."

This means "thirteen-year-old African American female. Urgent."

This is how the messages usually show up in my foster parents from a private California Facebook group. I see multiple posts like this a week: "15 y/o Caucasian male (she/her), basic rate, not known behaviors" or "13 y/o AA male, likes sports, watches inappropriate videos on cell." Just like that.

Julianna had added a bit more context to this particular email. "Thirteen-year-old African American female. Urgent. Her name is Naomi. Foster parents going to Los Angeles on vacation. Respite needed for the holiday weekend." She always tries to match the child with the right foster family, to increase the chances of permanency. In this case, she had sent it to the full list of foster parents in our agency, which left me wondering if there was something more.

After Lucy left, we were just doing respite, which is when you give other foster parents a break. Some respite cases could be because children are transitioning from one home to the next and the social worker hasn't found the right placement yet. For whatever reason, they can't stay in the original home.

The kids, Steve and I thought it was a great way to help while we healed and gauged what age worked better for our family.

Before and during Lucy's stay with us, we had been doing monthly respite for a now fourteen-year-old girl. She had become an extended member of our family, and we saw her frequently.

I reread the email and still wasn't sure why they disclose race, age, and nothing else. As if you could capture the essence of a person in two nondescriptive lines.

Steve saw the email before I had a chance and came to the bedroom. "Read Julianna's email."

"Of course we can do it!" I said after reading it quickly. "Did you respond already?" I asked assuming he had.

"Absolutely not without asking and discussing if it's a good fit!"

"That's so sweet! I think it will work. It's only a weekend. I'll let Julianna know."

I emailed Julianna immediately, and she must have been attached to her cell phone because not one minute went by and I got a note saying, "Thank you. You're awesome. Coordinate with Shonna, please."

"Shonna, is this a good time?" I asked after the phone rang for way too long to be a good time.

"Of course it is," Shonna replied.

I wonder how many of these calls catch her in a good time. How could there ever be a good time for her or any social worker? According to Walden University, in its article "Five Ways High Caseloads Hinder Social Work," county social workers are even more strapped, since their caseloads are between twenty-four and thirty-one kids at any given time and the recommended number is fifteen. The job of a social worker is remarkable and not properly supported. The whole system needs to be strengthened, including support for our social workers.

"Naomi is coming over to our house for respite," I told Shonna over the phone.

Shonna said, "Aww, thank you so much CarmenMaria. We really appreciate it."

"Is there anything I need to know?" I always ask this question, always fearing the kind of surprises you can get, even if it's only for a few days.

"I'll text you Elena's phone number. She's the foster mother, and you guys can connect on the details," she said.

At face value, you wouldn't make much out of that comment. But that seemingly innocent answer, the cryptic response in these types of cases, most likely means there are some issues.

If it's something really bad, it will only be for a few days... We can handle it... Let's hope it's not, though.

Elena and I arranged to have her drop off Naomi at 4 p.m. that Friday before the long holiday weekend.

"Elena, I've never hosted an African American teenage girl. Could you please help me out? We have a pool, and we're going to spend the weekend hanging out. Is there anything I should know about her hair? Is there anything else I should know about her?"

I need to remember to call my Black friends to ask them for hair advice. Do I have any Black friends I feel comfortable asking about their hair? I don't. Not really. I don't think I have anyone to call. I am friendly to my Black coworkers, but I'm not really friends with them. This is bad. How could I not have Black friends? Am I racist? It's clear I'm definitely biased. It's going to be so weird if I call them out of the blue to ask about hair. I need to do better.

"Have you had an African American kid before?" she asked.

I'm sure her tone was fine, but I felt I was being scolded for not being diverse enough, for not opening up our home to kids of color, for not having any close Black girlfriends to ask about hair. We were open to hosting any race and in our process of becoming foster parents, we had committed to ensuring kids from different races or cultures maintained their ties to their heritage. But at the moment, why is it the first thing I thought of was the hair? How has the cultural identity of this girl been reduced to this? At that point that was my only concern, and I felt so inadequate and utterly unprepared.

According to the National Conference of State Legislators, in 2018, "Black children were 13.71 percent of the population, yet 22.75 percent of the children in foster care." Their research calls out the disparities in the system toward the poor, as well as biases toward minorities.

I was unsure if calling out race was detrimental or beneficial. If the fact the system has race as a main descriptor at every step of the way, from removal to placements to services, has impacted the higher number of Black children being in foster care. If we didn't have race as a descriptor, would it be different? Would it be more in line with the population?

Or is it that it's being called out so they find a family who, regardless of the race, has the right cultural training and the child feels more at ease? Why isn't there any cultural training then?

Had we hosted any Black kids? Teo... sweetheart... such a long time ago, but how could I forget you?

"A Black boy, a while ago. He just stayed for a few days, and his hair was short," I replied. *And I was so ignorant about what he needed*, I should have added.

"You don't have to worry about it. She has a wig, and she knows how to handle her hair. I'll ask her if she would like to go to the pool. She doesn't have a bathing suit, but maybe we can stop at Target on the way there and get her one," she said.

I'm so glad I don't have to worry about the hair! The food may be easy... but the hair would have been tough.

"Any particular food she likes to eat? What does she like doing? Any rules I should be aware of? Bedtime, screen time?" I asked.

"She's picky. We will get a few foods she likes before we drop her off." She lowered her voice and said, "We're just a normal family, you know. We like spending time together, eating together, just the normal things, like a normal family... but she just stays in her room all day and doesn't want to hang out or even eat with us."

The change in tone and detailed information surprised me. "I see... Maybe she just needs a little time to adapt," I replied, matching her whisper.

"That's what we thought too. But she's been with us for a bit over a month, and she doesn't want to engage in any family activity. We thought it was because she's new to the system. We're her first placement. We planned this vacation before she arrived. And we *did* invite her. We asked her many times, but she doesn't want to come with us. We were even thinking of canceling. But we've paid a lot of money already. And my husband gave her a deadline and she said no. We kept asking, but *she* did not want to come. We want her to be part of our family. We wanted to adopt, you know. We had two little boys we thought we would keep, and they went back home. We miss them... We're just not bonding with her."

Wow, that's a lot to take in.

"It's okay; maybe she just needs a bit more time, and we all need vacations. You can't cancel. She will be fine," I reassured her.

Are all foster parents inclined to overshare and give explanations when things are not working out? Do we all just fear being judged? Or as foster parents, are we *actually* being judged? I think we are. I have endured questions after Lucy left such as "Wouldn't it have been better if she stayed with you?" or "Aren't transitions awful for them?" or even worse, "Why do you want to foster if you're not willing to keep her?"

I feel foster parents are always under such scrutiny, and we're so misunderstood that I'm constantly in "explanation" or "defense mode." A few times, I've realized I went out of my way to proactively explain why Lucy *had* to leave and how it wasn't really our fault.

Perhaps it's that we judge ourselves as well. I really wasn't judging Elena. I have no right to judge. As foster parents, the situations we go through are often extremely difficult and we're not fully prepared for them.

And I have to remind myself we didn't fail with Lucy. We show up, we are here, doing this job, again and again. I need to recognize sometimes, it just doesn't work out. I need to stop judging myself too harshly and forgive myself because I did try. And that's not failing.

CHAPTER 27

NOT YOUR FAULT

—

If you have been a victim of sexual assault and need help, call 800.656.HOPE (4673) to be connected with a trained staff member from a sexual assault service provider in your area or go to https://www.rainn.org/

Trigger warning: graphic content and sexual violence

The second Naomi arrived, I knew it was going to be hard.

She looked around and didn't say anything. I extended my hand and said, "Welcome. I'm CarmenMaria. Let me show you your room for the weekend."

"What's your name again?" she asked.

"CarmenMaria," I said.

"Can I call you Carmen?"

"Thank you for asking, but no... You can call me CM, Aunt, Tia, or CarmenMaria—just not Carmen," I replied. "Come with me. Do you need any help with your bag?"

She shook her head and grabbed her navy-blue duffel bag, purse, blanket, and pillow. So refreshing not to see garbage bags.

I left her alone to unpack and went downstairs to meet Elena and her husband. We headed out to the patio, and she handed me the large black binder. Similar to the one I had for Lucy...

My heart tightened. Grief comes in waves. You would be fine one second, and it hits you. Those memories are triggered so unexpectedly. The littlest thing would become a punch to my heart. I need to be mindful it happens the same way with the foster kids. An apparently innocent item, a black binder for me, would be painful.

"Thank you for having her this weekend. We will have our phones handy, and you can call anytime," she said. Her husband stayed quiet.

"She has asthma, and here is her medication. She knows how to use it herself, and she only takes it as needed. Here are the instructions," she said as she pointed at a specific section in the binder.

"Thank you," I replied, not knowing what else to say.

"We brought her some food. She's having trouble eating. Oh, and I usually take her cell phone away at 9 p.m."

Naomi opened the back door, came to us, and interrupted, "Can I come and live here? This is a nicer house. Can I live here?"

The air around us became heavy.

Elena's eyes widened. She looked at me silently and waited for me to respond. I remembered her words from the prior day: *We're not bonding.*

My mind raced. *What is the right answer for this question? I should have a plan. How do I tell her "no" without making*

her feel not wanted? And without making Elena feel inade-
quate or her home is not enough?

"That's not up to me, sweetheart."

Elena quickly added, "That's not something foster parents decide. You will have to call your social worker."

I'm thinking of Shonna and all the social workers who have to give answers that constantly disappoint these kids.

"But if you could, if you could keep me, would you want me?" Naomi insisted.

Quickly, think! And I rushed to respond, "Of course; any-one would want you. But it's not up to me. It's not up to your foster parents, and it's not even up to Shonna," I paused. "It's usually up to the judge."

Always blame the judge, someone told me once in training. And I have blamed the judge more times than I can count.

And just like that, Naomi turned around and went back into the house.

We looked at each other in awkward silence, so I asked Elena if instead of taking her phone at 9 p.m., I could ask Naomi to turn off the phone at 11 p.m. since it was a holiday weekend, and if I caught her using it after that time, I would ask her to give it to me. Elena agreed.

The husband didn't speak much. They both seemed uncomfortable. They thanked me and left.

I went upstairs, knocked on Naomi's door, and asked if we could talk for a bit.

She had picked the bed farthest from the door. I sat on the bed across from hers.

"Thank you for joining us for the weekend. I know it's a bit weird, but I would like to review a few house rules. It won't be long. I promise, I know... It's weird," I said.

She nodded.

I was hoping I wasn't coming on too strong. It's hard. I've heard of other foster parents who are a little bit more lenient for respite; others set up rules from the get-go. I don't know if there's a right way, so I was trying to feel her out but also thinking about my kids and how to ensure we are following the same rules, keeping everybody safe.

"It must be hard. Sorry. I just want to be on the same page; I will be quick."

She nodded.

"There are simple rules of respect: We don't hit, yell, or curse..."

Before I could finish, she jumped in. "If I'm on the phone with my friends and they cuss, it's not my fault. Elena says it's not my fault."

"Yep, you're right. It's not your fault, but if you are around the others, could you please take the phone off speaker so our youngest doesn't hear it, or others like me? I personally prefer not to hear it. Could you please help me with that?"

She nodded, guarded.

"Good, thank you. We also pick up after ourselves... like no garbage on the floor. And if you drop something, please just pick it up."

Nod.

"I know you have a cell phone and you hand it to Elena at 9 o'clock."

"Yeah, that sucks!" She raised her voice. "They treat me like a baby! I'm not their daughter. I'm in high school, and I don't like anyone touching my things. It's my phone. They didn't buy it for me. My mom bought it. It's *my* phone!" she started yelling.

"Got it. Your phone. What I was going to say is in this house we go to bed a little later, and I don't want to have to ask you to give it to me. Maybe while you're here it could be a bit different," I offered.

She just looked at me without saying anything, so I continued, "Since you're in high school, you must be responsible. And because it's summer vacation, you can keep your phone for the night, but please promise me you will turn it off by 11 p.m. I won't come and check. I will just trust you. Quiet time is at eleven anyway because I need to go to bed since I wake up early for work. You don't need to go to bed; please just don't be loud. The only condition is if I suddenly wake up in the middle of the night because you were loud on your phone, then at that time please hand it to me. I will return it the next day. Does that sound fair? But I think we will be fine."

Nod.

Phew! I don't know what I would have done if she said no... I need to think about how I share the house rules clearly and practice responses.

"For family dinners, we try to hang out, so we sit at the table with no cell phones."

"I'm a very picky eater; I'm never hungry," she revealed.

"That's okay. Even if you don't eat, if it's okay, we would like you to participate at dinner. Is there anything you like to eat? I'm a pretty decent cook."

"I only like junk food," Naomi responded.

"I can make your favorite homemade meal, or maybe we can cook together. What would you like?" I wasn't planning on giving up.

"I don't know any homemade meals. I don't remember. I was homeless for five years, and I only eat beef jerky and Jack in the Box."

What! Homeless for five years! How come she is new to the system? Who took care of this girl while she was homeless? She's thirteen. Had she been homeless since she was seven?

Breathe in, breathe out. Keep your cool.

"I'm so sorry. That must have been really hard," I said.

"Yeah, it was, but I'm tough. I grew up in the ghetto. I had to grow up fast so I'm very mature." She raised her voice again.

"I'm sure you are. I can see you're very assertive," I said, trying to share something positive.

She stopped for a second and responded in a much calmer voice, "Thank you."

I looked at her rich dark skin and her long black straight hair, and I doubted I had picked the right stuff. I tried to be as vulnerable as I could: "One more thing. Truthfully, I didn't know what products to get for your hair or skin, so please take a look at what I left in the bathroom. If it doesn't work, we can go to Target and get what you need."

I had called a couple of colleagues for advice and read some online blogs from white moms raising Black girls, but I wasn't sure if I had purchased the right brands. And I had forgotten the silk pillowcase.

I thanked her for her time and left. A few minutes later, she came downstairs and asked if we could go shopping. I had definitely missed the mark.

She was great at Target.

We couldn't find a few things and she asked the attendant for help, and afterward we walked around the different aisles, just browsing and hanging out. Then she asked if she could get a pride t-shirt, which caught me by surprise, but I said, "Of course," without probing further. She first picked a pricey one, looked at the tag, and chose a cheaper one.

We left and drove in silence for a while. I had purposely picked a Target store twenty minutes farther out than the one I usually go to, so we could have extra time in the car. Based on my experience, sometimes prolonged silence makes the child want to "fill in the space" and they start sharing. It has happened with activities in which I don't look at the child directly, like driving, building a LEGO set, or making a puzzle. Somehow, they relax and open up.

She thanked me again, told me it was the first LGTBQ+ t-shirt she had owned and she liked girls.

According to the nonprofit Children's Rights, "a 2019 study found 30.4 percent of youth in foster care identify as LGBTQ and 5 percent as transgender, compared to 11.2 percent and 1.17 percent of youth not in foster care. LGBTQ youth are more likely to suffer from consistent harassment and abuse in foster care, juvenile justice settings, and homeless shelters." They also share around 40 percent of homeless youth identify as LGBTQ.

In some cases, foster kids don't even share their gender identity because of fear of further abuse. Sometimes, they're in care *because of it.* I've also known of some religious-based foster care agencies that won't take LGTBQ+ foster parents.

Our belief is every child deserves a loving home, no matter how they express their identity. That's why we picked to work with Koinonia Family Services, a foster care agency that shares our family values.

I was humbled this child was opening up and trusting me. "Oh, thank you for sharing. What pronoun do you use? I'm she/her."

She looked at me, surprised. "I like she/her and also they/them. Sometimes it's easier with she/her."

"But what do *you* prefer?" I asked.

"She/her is all right."

"Okay, let me know if you change your mind," I replied.

"I don't like boys," she said. "I don't like men or boys. I don't trust them."

I stayed quiet.

"They did things to me," she said.

"I'm sorry," I replied.

Nod. A bit more silence.

"What is the difference between molestation and rape?" she asked.

That burgundy book from my bookshelf came back to my mind... the faded gold letters... *Merriam-Webster*... I sadly know those definitions too well.

rape
Noun
\ ˈrāp \
Definition of *rape*

1. unlawful sexual activity and usually sexual intercourse carried out forcibly or under threat of injury against a person's will or with a person who is beneath a certain age or incapable of valid consent because of mental illness, mental deficiency, intoxication, unconsciousness, or deception—compare *sexual assault, statutory rape*

molest
verb
mo·lest | \ mə-ˈlest \
molested; molesting; molests
transitive verb

1. to make unwanted or improper sexual advances toward (someone) *especially*: to force physical and usually sexual

contact on (someone). "He was sent to prison for *molesting* children."

Children... child. She's a child.

I took a few deep breaths and explained as best as I could the definitions, trying to keep an impossible sense of normalcy. Because you have to. Because if by any chance they suspect you're judging them, you risk making them feel ashamed or embarrassed.

"I was molested then," she said, trying to pinpoint what had happened. Naming it.

Does naming it make it better?

"Neither one of them are good. Neither one should happen to children. Neither one is the kid's fault," I said.

"It is my fault. I really didn't mean for this to happen. It just happened. We were just kissing and his right hand got between my legs, and he just got himself in. I was wearing a dress because it was summer, and it was hot. I had just put on a little bit of makeup—just eyeliner, mascara, and lip gloss. I just wanted him to like me because I'm so ugly, but I should have worn pants... I should have worn pants! I should've said something... I really didn't want this, but I didn't say no. It really caught me by surprise. It happened so quickly. He just did it! I was not wearing pants. I didn't have time to say something."

I wasn't expecting her to share so openly.

"I'm so sorry. But no, sweetheart, it's not supposed to be that way. You don't need to say no. If you didn't say yes, if he didn't ask, then it's a no. He needed to ask you first. It doesn't really matter if you were wearing pants, a dress, or you were fully naked. It doesn't. He needed to ask. Did this happen a while ago? Did you tell your social worker?"

"Yes, I did tell them, and it happened a while ago."

How old was she when this happened? I hope she's not in touch with this person.

"I need you to believe me. Nothing you did gave him the right to do that. If you didn't say yes, then it's a no. And if it's a grown-up who did this, even if you said yes, it's always no. I'm sorry this happened to you."

"It's okay; it's not a big deal," she responded.

"It's not okay, sweetheart. It *is* a big deal. And it's *not* your fault. Thank you for sharing with me," I said.

Nod.

Silence. Strangely enough, it was less uncomfortable this time.

CHAPTER 28

SO MUCH MORE

Three days... I only have three days, maybe four or five, to connect, to have an impact, to be impacted. I hope it's enough.

Over the weekend, the hair and the pool became irrelevant. I am embarrassed now to think how this could have been my most important concern for that placement.

Naomi hadn't left her room or eaten much of anything beyond a few bites of teriyaki beef jerky. I don't even think she was drinking much water. I was starting to get worried.

I knocked at her door a few times a day, and I could hear her on the phone, lots of cursing. When we called her for dinner she came downstairs, looked at her plate, said she wasn't hungry, and went back to her room.

Gema invited her to make some chocolate-covered strawberries, thinking she might like that.

"Can I stay longer?" she asked.

"Well, the social workers don't work on Sundays, so let me call them on Monday. But it can't be long, maybe a couple more days. Our oldest kids are coming on Wednesday, and I need the room... but I will try for two more days," I replied.

I didn't want her to feel rejected, but I was starting to see why Elena was having trouble bonding. Naomi was polite but unengaged. I felt we were only a hotel. Room, food, DO NOT DISTURB sign.

And that's not why we foster. We foster to help, but it also needs to work for us. We want to build relationships. We want it to have meaning and not be just transactional.

On the other hand, we also need to meet the children where they are. Was I doing enough to meet her where she was?

"Why can't I live here?" she asked again.

"We've already talked about this. It's not up to us. We're only doing short-term because my family is coming over for a few months, and I will have no rooms available."

"I just don't like it there. They have very strict rules, and they don't respect my privacy. They're nice, but they treat me like a child. They want me to sit at the table even if I'm not hungry. I 'asked' my social worker if I can leave, but she don't answer."

Oh, honey, this is a nice family, and they only want what's best for you. How do I tell you life dealt you a bad set of cards, and it's not going to get any easier? It's going to get tougher if you don't make an effort. You are going to be labeled as difficult. It's gonna be even harder for you because the system is racially biased. And it really sucks, and it's not your fault. It's all screwed up.

The foster care system is not immune to racism; furthermore, it sheds a light on it. The Children's Bureau's April 2021 Child Welfare report draws attention to the systemic racial disproportionality and disparity of the system, across all major decision points: "African-American children spend more time in foster care and are less likely to reunify with their families, and compared with White children, they are less likely to receive services. In addition, African-American and American-Indian or Alaska-Native children are more likely than other children to be removed from their homes and to experience a termination of parental rights (TPR)."

"Sweetheart, every house has rules. We're taking it easy right now because you're only staying for a few days. Normally my rules are stricter than what you see. You may not like it here either," I replied.

I hadn't checked if she had been using the cell phone past 11 p.m. I was slacking on the only rule I had told Elena I would enforce. I didn't want to know if she had turned it off as promised. I didn't want to have to deal with setting consequences if she hadn't... "Pick your battles" is what Steve usually said.

And I had a bigger battle to pick... I was concerned about the bias this child would experience if she kept transitioning to more homes.

"Elena is a good person. She just wants you to be part of their family. The thing is, if you're in your room all the time and not interested in being with them at all, you're not giving them a chance. I know you don't want to be there. I know it sucks... I'm sorry, I can't even imagine what you've been through. But I'm a bit concerned. You're not eating, and you're in your room all day. At some point, you will need to make an effort to eat and to get to know them," I explained.

"I don't eat because I have an eating disorder. Because I hate my body. I mean no disrespect," she said.

"I see... I'm sorry." I paused, searching for the right words.

"You're beautiful, but if you're not eating, most likely you will get sick. How are you going to get better? Are you seeing a counselor?"

"I've had six counselors, and I don't like any of them. They don't get me, and so I'm not going back to see them."

"Okay, maybe we can look for the right counselor—not every counselor is a good fit—because we need to figure out a way for you to eat something. It's pretty scary if you're not eating," I said.

Nod.

No change though. She continued to spend all her time in the bedroom chatting with her friends. She didn't come out much—not to eat, not to hang out, not to do anything—despite multiple requests. We even planned family activities to make her feel more at ease, like s'mores over a fire pit one night.

Both my kids had started to complain. "Why did I have different rules for her than for them?" they asked. "Don't you say you have the same rules for everyone in the family? Don't you say every foster kid is part of the family? If she's part of the family, why can she do whatever she wants?" I had nothing to say to them and asked for a bit more patience.

I called the agency and Elena and got the approval for Naomi to stay a few more days.

"Naomi, could we talk for a second, please?" I knocked at her door, and she opened it. "I emailed the head of the agency asking if you could stay a couple of more days. They said yes. It has to be just two days, though. Remember my family is coming over." I figured I would start with the positive.

Her expression changed instantly. Her frown relaxed, her eyes teared up a bit, and her voice became softer.

"Thank you for wanting me," she said. "No one has ever wanted me. My dad don't want me; he left when I was three. My mom don't want me back. My social worker said she don't want me back. Thank you for wanting me."

How do you respond to that?

These children need to feel wanted, loved. Besides keeping them safe, our most important job as foster parents is to show them they're worthy of love, or they risk falling into the hands of predators and traffickers. Although she hadn't been trafficked to my knowledge, we've had other girls for respite who had been. Their low self-esteem fully played a role in it. That's why 60 percent of sex trafficking victims were in foster care, and I feel increasing their sense of worth is critical to prevent it (Miller, 2020). But how could I do that? How could I answer in a way that is empathetic but doesn't blame the biological family while building her confidence?

"Oh sweetheart, of course. I'm sorry for what you're going through. I'm sorry you can't go back to your mom," I responded, trying to avoid blaming anyone.

How do I approach the room and food? How do I reach her? I felt unprepared.

"I can see you're strong and resilient. You've gone through a lot and here you are. Still trying to make the best out of the situation. You're staying in touch with your friends through all of this; it seems you're a great friend. You're assertive. You say what you want in a very clear way. You've been very respectful with us and you're kind. I saw the way you treated Gema. You were very patient and kind with her when she was making the chocolate-covered strawberries," I shared.

She looked at me and whispered so quietly I almost missed it, "Thank you for saying that. No one has ever said those things to me."

"People don't know that side of you because you're staying in your room all day, and I'll bet it's because you're sad, but maybe you're also building a bit of a barrier," I added. "We're just trying to make you feel welcomed, and I would love to see if you could give us a chance, you know, we're trying."

"Yeah, you're nice, but I don't feel comfortable. I told you I grew up in the ghetto, in the streets, you know. You're the perfect White family. You play board games and watch TV together and have fun in the pool. But that's not for me. I don't watch the type of movies you watch, I don't eat what you eat, I don't speak the same way. This is not for me," she said.

I paused for a second. It was true, and it was hard to hear. We watched a movie with White actors, we made chocolate-covered strawberries, and we made s'mores on a fire pit. We are privileged. She was right. Our efforts to make her feel welcomed were the efforts of White people in a comfortable position intending to connect with her from *our* perspective, not trying to understand where she was in her life.

My next attempt to connect was still not ideal; I was asking her to behave differently versus trying to understand where she was coming from. "I see. I'm sorry we're making you feel uncomfortable. What can we do to make you feel better? I want to try, and I am also afraid if you don't try, you'll end up leaving Elena's house, going to a new house, and staying all day in your room not eating. Then you won't fit in again; you will go to another home, not fit in *again*, and another home... and you will end up in a group home, and you don't want that."

"I know, I don't want to be in jail again. I was just there, in juvie. I don't want to go back," she replied. "It was crap. I just left a month ago!"

WHAT? What do you mean in jail? Why don't they share more? This is exactly the issue! We try to be open, but I should have the right to know if I want to have a child who has been in juvie sleeping in the room next to my own child.

Was I scared because she had been in jail? How much was my bias impacting my anxiety?

"Oh, I can't even imagine what that was like," I said, trying to control my emotions... *Regulate... Regulate... Maybe there is a reason...*

By then, I'm judging, my guard came up while she was confirming my bias with every new piece of information, and a million thoughts flowed through my mind. *Are we safe? Could she be carrying drugs or weapons? I have a kid who's been in juvie, maybe doing drugs, sleeping in the room next to Gema. How do I know if this is safe for my family? How do I know if she's not involved in other stuff?*

In contrast, I was also thinking, *Did she go to juvie because she was Black? Are there mitigating circumstances I'm not seeing? Could I be judging too harshly? She's a child. What if she's a good kid, and I fail to see it? She may just need a break. This is so hard. Why isn't there more transparency and support? Why can't we address race in the system and the true impact it has on the possible outcome of these children. Can't we be better trained?*

"Thank you for being so open," was the only thing I could say, trying to stay calm, thinking maybe there were mitigating circumstances.

"You can ask me whatever you want, and I'll tell you," she said.

Let's hope there are mitigating circumstances...

"How come you ended up there?"

"Elderly abuse, the judge said. I'm not a bad person. My mamma kept beating me up with a belt, and one day I grabbed it and hit her back. But she called the cops on me. I never called the cops on her! I still love her, but she don't want me back."

"I'm so sorry sweetheart... You're right. I'm sorry. You don't want to go back to juvie or worse, end up on the streets, doing drugs," I added.

"No, I'll never do that shit again. Pardon ma mouth. I've been clean for more than a month."

I couldn't believe it! "13 y/o AA F" was such an inadequate description it was ridiculous.

Every little bit of information was equally heartbreaking and concerning. On one hand it was drugs, violence, jail. On the other, abuse, neglect, abandonment. I wanted to understand where she came from, while trying to keep my own bias in check.

My internal dialogue continued: *Give her a break. But this is so hard. I need to be open minded and say something positive fast!*

"You see! Over a month clean! That's amazing! Congratulations! You're strong and resilient. I can tell. I know it! Thank you so much for sharing. I think we should go and have frozen yogurt to celebrate progress? Maybe froyo is something you would eat?"

Nod.

And we did. Everybody came, as a white/Latino family with a thirteen-year-old Black child, doing our best to build bridges.

And she ate the full thing.

The next day the social worker found her a placement with a Black family, and Naomi came to tell me, "All my problems are gonna be solved."

"That's good, sweetheart. Keep in touch. Here is my cell phone number if you need me."

And off she went, and I stayed, reflecting on this experience. On the information needed to make a thoughtful decision about taking on a child with such a background. On how critical it is to know more so I can properly care and protect my bio children as well. On the system, its bias, and how it compares to mine. On how maybe this child had less chances because of her race. On how if I don't open my mind, I would miss this opportunity to learn, to empathize. On how foster care should be a better equalizer and intensely support minority children. And how we desperately need appropriate cultural training, so race is examined in the context of what the child needs to be successful.

I don't pretend to know much about this subject. This conversation needs much more attention, and I don't feel sufficiently educated. I'm personally just coming to grips with my own shortcomings, such as thinking hair is the only defining characteristic I should be concerned about. My friend and fellow author Amnoni L. Myers shares in her book *You Are the Prize*: "I was just a girl who went through the foster care system, navigating struggles that every Black person navigates." I encourage others to read her perspective as a foster care alumna.

Last time we texted, Naomi was doing well. She said she's happy, and they *get her*. She said she's eating.

When I said goodbye, I reminded her of what a great kid she was because they need to hear it often, so they can start believing it. Because she is so much more than that scarce description.

Thirteen-year-old STRONG, RESILIENT, RESPECTFUL, KIND, SMART, LOYAL FRIEND, CARING, BEAUTIFUL, BLACK YOUTH.

PART IV

REFLECTIONS

CHAPTER 29

OUTCOMES

"Danny is coming to visit. I talked with his dad last night," I said to Steve casually one night while watching TV.

It had been months since I had heard from Danny or his dad. It's not often we get the privilege to stay in touch with our foster kids, and I'm so grateful his dad and I still maintained contact. We usually sent birthday and Christmas wishes, and during those occasions, I scrolled down through their social media pages to see how he was growing up. *I haven't forgotten about you; I just love you from a distance.*

"How come?" Steve replied.

"Well..." I paused. "They're doing a road trip and wanted to know if they could all visit and stay with us for a week." Before Steve could even think about it, I said, "I told him absolutely, they're our family and they're welcome any time."

He smiled. "When are they coming?"

"In about a month and a half; the kids should be out of school, so we can take a few days off and hang out with them."

"Good." We both smiled, holding hands, my heart filled with joy.

During the next few weeks, I couldn't contain my excitement, which translated into me asking everyone to clean, tidy up, and clean some more. I was driving everyone crazy until the day arrived.

"I can't believe you're here!" I said euphorically, as I opened the door and saw Danny and his parents standing in our doorway after so many years.

Danny had grown so much! He was much taller, but he still had his sweet smile and his kind blue eyes. When he said, "Hi," I was surprised to hear his deeper voice—not the voice of the little kid he was once. Iago, Gema, and Steve were right behind me, pushing me away, and we all gave each other long hugs.

I couldn't believe the three of them were there, after so many years, after all we had gone through. *How is Danny feeling? How does he see me now?* He was my son in my heart, in my little jewelry box of memories. So many questions. *Did he still love me? Did he resent me? Was it awkward for him?*

That week was full of excitement: We went to San Francisco and got tickets for a boat ride at Fisherman's Wharf. We saw whales and got wet with the waves. We ate tons of junk food, played board games, and jumped in the pool every day, even at night. The kids played as if no time had gone by, and they all stayed up past their bedtime. The same late laughs as when they were little.

I even booked a double massage in my favorite local place for his mom and me to go together. That may have been a bit too much because they put us in a couple's room, and getting naked, even under the sheet, was not how I had planned to bond with her. Back at home, I cooked Peruvian food, and we simply had a great time—like old friends, like family.

~

"Remember Teo?" Iago asked Danny one night after we were done with dinner.

I remember Teo; I remember all my kids.

"Oh, yes!" said Danny. "Yeah... he was a cool kid."

"Oh, yeah, he was cool," added Iago. "Remember he got mad about his present that time?"

I had forgotten about the incident.

Teo had been in our home back in Chicago, when we were doing Safe Families, at the same time as Danny. We were originally not planning on adding anyone else, but one day we got a text from our social worker saying they needed urgent help. It was a domestic abuse situation. A mom and her three kids—Teo, who was ten, a three-year-old, and a three-month-old baby—were running away from the violent boyfriend, sleeping in their car. It was fall in the Midwest, and I could only imagine how cold those nights were. Teo's mother and grandmother had grown up in the foster care system and had no support. Safe Families was called, and they found homes for all children, but the family taking Teo was unfortunately out of town, so they needed someone to cover for a week.

I picked him up that same night from a maroon Chevy in a sketchy neighborhood. He was wearing a visibly small t-shirt, dirty jeans, and no socks. I knew he was hungry, so I asked if he wanted to grab McDonald's right away and stop at Target, but he replied, "Can I get a sweater first, please?"

I gave him my jacket, stopped for a full meal, and went to Target to buy all the basic items. As I remember that trip, I'm embarrassed to share how poorly I handled it. We should have been in and out of there, but instead, I asked him about his favorite color and lightly quizzed him on which item was a better value. *What was I thinking?* This kid was hungry and in distress, and in my nervousness, I couldn't think of better ways to break the ice.

During the week or so he stayed with us, he was very kind to Gema, and I guessed he was extremely caring with his siblings too. He was friendly with Iago and Danny, although he had issues with Steve as a male authority figure.

We found out his birthday had recently passed, and he hadn't celebrated, so one night we bought him a scooter, a helmet, and pads. The items were so big we put them inside an empty dollhouse box. We sat at the table to eat dinner followed by cake. We sang "Happy Birthday" and gave him the present. His eyes opened wide. He started unwrapping, and he saw the doll house box. He stood up in rage, threw the present to the floor, yelled "Are you making fun of me?" and stormed out of the room.

We didn't expect his reaction. We all followed him and said we couldn't figure out how to wrap it, so we put it all in this empty box. It took some convincing, but he calmed down, finally opened the present and lowered his head. "No one has ever given me anything like this... thank you."

We kept seeing Teo once he went to his next Safe Family. He came to our birthday parties, I saw him at parks, and I tried to keep in touch. He stayed with Bridgette—his Safe Family mom—for about nine months and through that period, she discovered he had been beaten up by the boyfriend, left in a room with his siblings and a bag of Doritos for full weekends, all while the mom and the boyfriend did drugs.

Eventually, the bio mom got help, moved to another town where Teo got to stay with another Safe Family, who loved them all—him, the mom, his siblings—without reservations or judgment, with extreme tolerance. They loved them radically. That new Safe Family became the miracle they needed. It took some time, but his mom is now healthy, married to a nice man, had another baby, and now they're able to break the dreadful cycle of foster care outcomes.

Usually, 20 percent of foster youth aging out are automatically homeless and half of them become homeless before age twenty-four, with only 3 percent graduating from college, and 25 percent convicted of a crime (Balistreri, 2021). I was so glad Teo's future had a better outlook than those statistics.

I was lost in my train of thought reflecting on Teo's story when Iago brought me back to the moment and asked me, "Mommy, *what* happened to Teo? Do you know?"

"Oh, yes! He's doing well! He's a three-sport athlete: football, basketball, wrestling. He gets at least Bs, works full time, and bought himself a car. He spent a week this summer with Bridgette, his other Safe mom," I told the boys.

"That's good," Iago responded. Danny nodded, not realizing the significance of this accomplishment.

The relationship Teo built with Bridgette's family and his next Safe Family had a positive impact. He went from sleeping in an old Chevy to having a promising future.

And Danny's outcome: He was back with his parents, safe, healthy, loved. We had done our job. That's how you want the end to be.

Where would Naomi end up? Or Lucy? Could I be hopeful for their potential future? In their cases, they couldn't go back home, and it wasn't clear what was to come for them. Danny was the same age as Lucy when we had him. Did he remember how much we loved him? If he remembers, can I assume Lucy would remember? That would give me hope.

I wanted to ask Danny a myriad of questions and tell him how important he was for me, but I was concerned about ruining things. And before long, they were gone. And I was left with all these feelings stuck in my throat, words left unsaid.

He will never know how much he means to me.

~

Some time went by, and I texted his dad one day: "Can we talk? I'm writing a book about our foster care experience, and I would love to connect with you. In full transparency, there are a few chapters about Danny."

What was he going to say? I had changed the names, and I had not disclosed any identifying information, but still. What if they got mad at me and it damaged our relationship? What if it hurt them? What if reading it caused additional trauma?

He didn't respond to my text immediately. I became a bit anxious. Sharing the story of Teo and Danny in the book has become essential in how I process my feelings of hope for Lucy, even Naomi. Different kids, I know, but somehow, they have become an analogy of their future. It gives me a bit of closure thinking Lucy may find happiness in a forever home someday, whichever home that is.

He finally texted me back: "Monday is a holiday; we have time."

"Excellent," I replied, nervously.

CHAPTER 30

FOSTERLY LOVE

———

Both Danny and his dad were on the video call. I wasn't prepared to see Danny. He had grown even more since he visited.

I took a deep breath and began. "Hi! It's good to see you both. Thank you very much for being here. This is so weird, and I don't know how to start. I guess I'll start with saying I love you, Danny. You will always have such a special place in our hearts, and it was an honor to have you in our home when we did."

He nodded, not saying anything. He seemed a bit uncomfortable, unsure if it was due to the unusual circumstances or the memories. Who could blame him? I felt the same way.

I turned my eyes to his dad, avoiding looking at Danny, and said, "And it was an honor you named us as godparents."

This had been a big deal. We were not registered as foster parents when we were in Chicago—just volunteers of Safe Families. When a child enters the foster care system, he would've had to go into a licensed home or to a family member as a kinship placement (a placement with a relative). Danny's parents chose us as their family when they named us godparents, which allowed us to keep him without meeting the full requirements of traditional foster homes. The county gave us a grace period to formally get certified and meet the requirements of kinship fostering.

More nods, no words…

How do I say all the things I want to say? I'm just going for it. Looking at Danny, I said, "I know I shared a little bit about the book I'm writing and how difficult it was when our last foster daughter left. It was a heartbreaking decision. And it was different than when you left because you were going back home. We knew we were going to miss you, but we were at peace because we did our job."

He didn't answer and looked at me intensely. I was treading carefully, trying to choose the right words. I didn't want him to think we didn't feel anything when he left and I also wanted him to know we were happy he went home, that both feelings can coexist. I added, "Don't get me wrong. I had a lot of mixed feelings when you left, and the kids did too. You and Iago were like siblings. And with Gema. Do you remember Gema would say 'ma boys'? So funny," I paused. *And you were "ma boy," too.*

Danny shared a hint of a smile and said, "Yeah, when I first got to be at your house, it kind of sucked because I was away from everybody, but eventually I kind of grew into another family. Gema and Iago were a little sister and brother."

His dad started talking. "Yeah, I remember Gema's voice; she was so little." He paused and added in a more ominous tone, "But those times were the hardest of my life. I hated you. I really hated you."

Hard to swallow. I didn't know he had such strong feelings toward me, but I also wasn't in his shoes.

"It must have been awful, having your son removed and not being able to do anything about it," I replied, trying not to make it personal. I was making a true effort to listen with the intent of understanding.

"It's the worst feeling in the world. You obviously want to get your son back, so I *had* to play the game because if I didn't, I wouldn't get him back."

I couldn't even imagine. He first lost one son to a disease they didn't know he had, and Danny was removed while the police investigated the death of his first child, which took ten long months. I don't know if I would have been able to survive.

"I can't even imagine. Basically, you lost two children at once. How did you even handle it?"

"I'm still handling it because I still hold so much ill will toward everyone who did that to us," he replied.

I turned to Danny and said, "And from our point of view, the only thing we knew was your brother had died and your parents were under investigation. We had so many mixed feelings. We saw you were such a good kid, so it became evident good people raised you. We didn't know what to believe. We wanted you to stay in touch with your parents, but we were also extremely concerned about your safety and our kids' too." Looking now at his dad, I added, "And somehow, through all of that, we managed to build a relationship."

His dad agreed, "We did. I think it probably started when we went door to door selling popcorn for the Boy Scouts. When I finally got to walk around and talk with you. We had an actual, legitimate conversation. And I saw you wanted Danny to just be a child, to be in sports, to be a normal kid. You were trying to give him as much of a normal life as you could. So yeah, our relationship really changed on the day of the popcorn sale."

And then he revealed something that completely caught me off guard. "But it was really hard. I mean, I've already told you. When he first came to live with you, you sent me a picture of the lemonade stand, and I could see the partial street name. I went to Google Earth and found the exact location of your house. And that night I drove over. I was outside staring at the red door for hours, debating if I should get in and snatch Danny out."

I looked at him in disbelief and couldn't say anything. Danny looked at him as well.

"Oh, yeah. I debated for hours what to do. I could've snagged him, and I could've taken off. But who knows how far I would've gotten? And if I screwed up and they caught me, I knew I wouldn't be able to see him 'til he was eighteen, so after hours of torture, I went back home."

What? I'm so glad I never knew!

"No! You never told me," I heard myself saying with a higher tone than intended. "I had no idea. I would have called the police if I'd known. It could have been a tragedy. I would've confirmed what the social worker hinted, you were a criminal. It would have been a disaster." *This isn't going as planned.*

"Well, we didn't know who you were either. We didn't know if you were just in it for the money, you know what I mean," his dad justified.

"Did you know Safe Families don't get paid? That we were volunteers? We don't do this for the money!" I was starting to get a bit irritated, trying to justify my intentions.

"I didn't know... But I knew some people are there for the money; they don't care about the kids. It's a moneymaker; it's like human trafficking from the parents' side."

That's another problem. Foster care has such a bad reputation. Lori Groves and James Kenny in their article "Criminalizing Foster Parents" shared, "Foster care receives negative publicity. Children may be threatened: 'If you don't behave, we will have to send you to a foster home.'" I also hear "You're one of the good ones" and it annoys me. The system is all around broken, there is such a lack of transparency, and everyone is suspicious of each other.

I'm not denying abuse happens at the hands of foster parents. The Children's Bureau of the US Department of Health and Human Services reports 0.7 percent of the abuse happens in the care of foster parents, guardians, or group homes. I personally think it's much more, and it's just under-reported. One of my foster children shared her prior foster mom used to beat her up with wooden spoons on the back of her feet and she never told anyone. It's truly awful adults who are supposed to take care of vulnerable children abuse them.

On the other hand, I have also witnessed other foster parents, child advocates, and social workers, like Shonna, Julianna, and Jerry from my agency, truly care for the children and try to make things better. I feel the need to speak for many foster parents whom I've had the privilege to interact with: *We do this because we care.*

I took a breath. *He thought about it, but it never happened. We're here now. Focus on the present and our relationship today,* I told myself. "Glad you didn't break into my house! I got to know you better on Halloween. I remember it was very cold, snowing, and we were walking around with you guys, and I was thinking, *I should've stayed home,* but I genuinely wanted to get to know you."

"It was raining slush," Danny said. We all laughed. The tension dissipated, and he added, "Yeah, and we had dinner at home. Those were awkward."

Did I hear right? He said home—dinner at home.

His dad jumped in, "Awkward to say the least. Because I didn't know you, and I had to sit in *your* house and not do what I wanted to do with *my* son. He is my life. And my life was in someone else's house. That's one of the hardest feelings."

"I can't even imagine what you were going through. For us it was difficult. The visits I have today with my foster children's parents are different from the ones we had with you. They are supervised and mostly in an office. In the case of Lucy, my former foster daughter, we dropped her off on one side of a building, and her parents came in through the opposite side, through a completely different door. We didn't have to interact with them at first. It was very unusual for you to come over to our house to visit Danny weekly and by no means required."

I know he was angry and he resented me, but it wasn't our fault. I wanted him to know we made a true effort to build a relationship and to connect with them. Although I know of families who build a strong relationship with the child's bio family, not everyone is open to bringing them into their homes weekly, with no supervision. Some people may consider this pretty risky. Even Lucy's social worker thought it was safer not to give Lucy's mom our contact information; everything had to be done through her.

Thankfully, Danny jumped in, breaking the tension. "I don't remember much, but I do remember Iago and Gema comforted me, especially at night after watching *Wreck-It Ralph*."

Oh my goodness, he remembers! "Those nights were heart-breaking," I admitted.

"Now Danny is much older, I need to confess 99 percent of the time I didn't have *Wreck-It Ralph* on. I just faked it and went, 'Oh, no. Oh wait, right now,'" his dad confessed.

"Oh wow! I had no idea!" I exclaimed.

"Me neither," Danny laughed.

How could we laugh about this? But we were. We were laughing.

I turned to Danny. "There is something I would like your opinion on. I've talked with a couple of guardians ad litem, who are like lawyers representing the kids, and a CASA worker. CASA stands for Child-Appointed Special Advocate, and they're volunteers looking out for the kids in foster care. I asked them what's better: having kids in the house when you foster or not? They said no, the children who come into a home are better off with no other kids in the family, so they can get the full attention from the foster parents. What do you think?"

Danny looked at me, and without hesitation, he answered, "Well, if you are giving the option to go into a foster family who has kids or no kids, I would say with kids. It's a lot easier to relate to them, instead of being with these new adults who you have no idea who they are, and you don't trust."

"That's what I thought," I said. But then, I wondered about Lucy. She definitely needed the full attention of the parents, and I think she would benefit from having no other children in her new home. But maybe, if we would've gotten more support to start and help throughout, the outcome may have been different. I still think it's generally beneficial to have permanent children in the home. We just need to be more aware of how children with trauma affect them.

I was also curious of what Danny thought of us after these many years. "And when you left, how was it to go back to your home after you had been with us for so long?" I asked him.

"Well, it was definitely weird going back to my own room, my own house, but what helped me through it was everybody here was so welcoming," he responded.

I decided to go for it: "And now, after these years, how do you see us?" I thought of him, of the other kids, of Lucy.

"I mean, if we ever go to California again, we're definitely stopping by to see you guys. It was... it is ... you guys are really close to us. We may not talk every day, but the love is there," he said and chuckled.

After so many years, after everything that happened, love is truly there, my sweetheart, my son.

love
noun
\ ˈləv \
Essential meaning of *love*
   1. a feeling of strong or constant affection for a person
motherly/maternal *love*
fatherly/paternal *love*

I should suggest to *Merriam-Webster Dictionary* to add:
"Fosterly: When a foster parent loves their foster child as their own, even though he may never know it."

CHAPTER 31

FOSTER COURAGE

"Do you think we're ready for more than respite? Do you think both kids will be okay?" I asked Steve. He didn't answer.

It had been over six months since Lucy left. We had continued to do respite for Isabel, the fourteen-year-old who had been coming monthly since before having Lucy, and who fit with our family really well.

Recently, Shonna and Jerry organized a trauma training directed to the permanent children in the foster families at the agency. They taught what causes trauma and the expected behaviors from foster kids. Both Gema and Iago now understood why Lucy behaved the way she did. Although it was great progress, I thought it was insufficient. Regardless of if they understood or not where the kids' behaviors came from, it was our duty to keep our children safe, and I wanted to ensure they were part of our decision making if we were to start longer-term placements.

It had to be different this time or we wouldn't be able to foster again.

I had been reading about secondary trauma, and I was convinced if it affects social workers, teachers, it had a similar impact or even worse on foster families. If so, why is it not spoken about? I had no doubt Gema had suffered from listening to Lucy's stories about her dad, as well as suffering from her direct attack (this wasn't secondary). Fortunately, we had been going to therapy and things had gotten better, but Steve and I had to rethink our approach, make meaningful changes from how we handled things to who we accepted at our home.

Reflecting on the impact, I felt Iago had been mostly ignored. Through the whole Lucy stay and the aftermath, he had been seemingly alright, but I kept wondering if our focus on Gema had made us miss something in him. I learned the term "glass children," which refers to a child whose parents are focused on another child in the family who needs their full attention, due to medical or mental health issues. They called them glass kids because the parent sees right through them instead of attending to their needs (RADSibs, 2022).

I had to make sure I was not missing anything with Iago.

~

"Do you remember when Danny left? Was it hard?" I asked Iago one day when I picked him up from a baseball game. We had never talked about it, and I felt guilty it didn't occur to me how he felt. I had been focused solely on my grief back then and not on him.

"Yeah, I was a little emotional for a few days after he left. He was basically like a cousin." He paused and continued, "More like a brother. We were basically brothers. We played together. We did everything together. I think of him as my brother. It was weird because I was bummed but happy at the same time. Sad, but kept thinking he needed to go back home. Imagine if you were a child and you got taken away from your biological family. Imagine that. Your childhood is ruined."

It was eye-opening to learn how he had the same mixed feelings at age seven as I did as an adult. I wondered if he had suffered with Lucy too.

"Lucy was tough. Were you okay with her? What should we do differently next time?" I asked him.

"Well, when she joined our house, I had privacy, but Gema didn't. We didn't think about her. It's like if someone asked you and Dad if you would share a room with a stranger for an indefinite time. Would you feel comfortable?"

Before I could answer, he continued, "No, you wouldn't. Wouldn't you want privacy? Yes, you would. Lucy was a stranger to all of us when she came." The way he said it, such obvious truth, hit me.

In many foster parent-related moments—training, articles, blogs, online support groups—there is the notion we're strangers to the foster children. That the child coming to our home has been removed from the places they know, from family and friends, and placed with strangers. It's true. However, it wasn't until Iago said it so bluntly I realized the children coming into our care are strangers too, and we're asking *our* children to willingly share their space, their parents' time, and their lives with strangers. Although they're all kids, they don't know each other. We expect more from them than from ourselves. We would never ask our spouse to bring another adult into our bedroom and be okay with it. Why do we expect this from our children? Why do we think they would be resilient, and what they give up doesn't matter?

"Do you think it's better for the children to come into a home with kids or with no kids?" I asked, trying to grasp if he wanted to continue being a foster family, because so far, it wasn't looking that good.

"I'll give you an example. You went to school, didn't you? Would you rather go with a teacher and just you, or have students there too?" He looked at me, but this was another of his questions where he didn't expect an answer, so he went on. "Yep. And if the teacher is not very good... Imagine that!"

I smiled. He was so, so logical.

"Are there any advantages of having foster kids?" I kept digging.

"The advantage for the kid is to make them feel welcomed and they're part of the family. That is our job. That is the goal."

"But what are the benefits of having foster kids for *you*, *amor*? Are there any?" I emphasized. Was there any?

"When I grow up and I'm a man, I want to know I made them feel better about themselves because they were in a family. They met people they could actually trust. I think the advantage is I personally get to know what they're going through and help them. Or at least I hope I help them. And that's just beautiful."

My baby, you are becoming an amazing man. "I'm always so proud of you," I said, but at that precise moment, the depth and thoughtfulness of his response gave me infinite pride. He was better than okay.

~

The next day I took Gema for frozen yogurt at our favorite place. I needed to be delicate on my approach and not exert *any* pressure. "*Amor,* you know Daddy and I have been talking about bringing other kids at some point, but we want to make sure you and Iago are on board. How are you feeling about it?"

"Lucy was very tough, *Mami*. She was more than I could manage."

"I know, *amor*. I'm sorry. She was more than *I* could manage, more than we were ready as a family to manage. Not every kid will be that way, but I want to know if you want us to foster again, or if we need to wait longer."

"If you want to do it, *Mami*...," she said hesitantly.

"No, *amor*. We all have to want to do it. It's okay to say no. I won't be mad at all. I really, *really* want to know how you feel."

She took another bite of the frozen raspberry yogurt and replied with her full mouth. "It depends on the age, their personality, and how the relationship is gonna go. So if a foster kid is really cool and chill like Danny or Isabel, yes. Some foster kids are angry, and they release all their anger on somebody... on someone who does not have a lot of power... like me. Then it's a lot. I feel bad for them because they have experienced a lot of trauma, but their anger comes toward me and it hurts."

I loved she had understood the training and at least Isabel and Danny were positive experiences, but she was right. Lucy had released her anger at her. I was also concerned we wouldn't know for sure how the foster child was going to react until we had them in our home. We would never have certainty it was the right fit. But we would try to ask as many questions as possible, but the answers will always lack the necessary information. Lucy was supposed to fit perfectly well on paper.

I took one bite of my frozen yogurt and nodded. She continued, "I thought Lucy was going to be really nice and we were going to be friends at the end, but she kept releasing all her anger on me, and I just wanted to be left alone."

It was true. She had tried, and Lucy did too.

I replied, "It was hard. You can always tell us if you need time alone, time with us, or if you don't feel you got enough help from us. It's okay to do that. I'm sorry we didn't help you enough." I was still sorry to have missed how much she had struggled. "So do you still want to have foster kids in the house? It's okay to say no."

"I want somebody older than me, maybe, easier to cope with. But I'm okay with a baby. You may have to forgive the baby when they are throwing stuff at you or touching your things because they are babies. But someone like six, seven... if they attack you, that's not okay," she stated.

"Is there anything good for you about having foster kids? Any benefit for you?" I wanted to make sure she wasn't saying that out of guilt or out of her need to make me happy.

"I sometimes like having foster kids because I like making people happy. I like to help them, it makes me feel good," she replied with her mouth full.

"What should we do better next time, so it doesn't become this hard?" I was really probing.

"I need my own room. Maybe every once in a while, check up on me, you and me alone, and talk. We can work on a code, like 'guitar,' so if I say 'guitar' it means I need help without them knowing I'm talking about them. We can't have someone who takes their anger out on me."

"That won't happen again," I said in agreement. "Is there anything you like about fostering?"

"When I was being nice, my heart was like exploding with love. When you're making someone else happy, you get a warm feeling in your heart."

Yes, amor, you do. You and your brother are really one of a kind (more like two of a kind).

"I need to focus, *Mami*. My froyo is melting. You're not eating yours either." She took a few more bites and cleaned the side of the cup that was spilling.

~

And then Steve. Anything we decided, he was the one who carried the most weight. Ultimately, I went to work outside the home, and he was—and is—the one who runs this family, taking the kids to their appointments, dropping and picking up kids from schools, writing reports, managing visits, dealing with the daily behaviors, and most importantly, bonding with the children. He's the one who quietly goes with the flow, willing to take in any child who needs us, more generous with his time than I could ever be.

I felt much more aware of my children's feelings, and I knew things were going to be different, but was he also ready? Was the family ready? When was the time the grief subsided enough to give room for hope?

"I chatted with both kids, sweetheart. I think it will be alright if we change a few things. I think I am okay to start over. But how about you? Are you also ready?" I asked him, curiously.

He turned to me, and with his incredibly kind heart, he said, "Should we tell Shonna we're open for business?"

That next day, I woke up reciting this verse of the poem from Antonio Machado: *"Caminante no hay camino, se hace camino al andar,"* which translates to "Traveler, there is no road; you make your own path as you walk."

There's no clear path, no perfect walkway, no streetlights illuminating the way. There is just the courage to take the first step, to observe if the soil is firm, to adjust and take the next step, to adjust and take another step, to venture into the journey, and to create a path of hope.

As I made my espresso that morning while Steve packed lunchboxes, I said, "I'll give Shonna a call today. I will ask her to revise the age ranges a bit and be more mindful about the background and questions we ask."

He looked at me, smiled, and nodded. "Please tell Shonna no more than two!" He was excited.

I agreed. "Okay, let's keep it simple until Gema and Iago are a little bit older. I'll have a couple of friends at work who are not having any more kids and have offered to give me their baby things."

"Sounds like a plan," said my man of few words, and he took off to take the kids to school.

I called Shonna that same morning during a break in a meeting. I don't know why I was a bit nervous, but she told me not to worry about it. She would make sure the full team was aware of what Gema and Iago had said and about age ranges. We would have our regular home inspection, which was due in a few weeks, and she wanted to talk with the kids again to make sure they were on board. We also had to resubmit our insurance cards, driver's licenses, and car registration, which apparently were expiring. It was reminiscent of our start.

It would seem we're ready to walk alongside one another, holding each other's hands tightly, willing to adjust after every step, and to create our own path together. We were ready, after all.

Foster Courage

Adjective

fos·ter | \ ˈfȯ-stər , ˈfä- \

Noun

cour·age | \ ˈkər-ij , ˈkə-rij \

Mental or moral strength to love whoever is entrusted to us, for as little or as long as needed, knowing our heart could be broken so theirs can heal, and do it willingly over and over.

EPILOGUE

"CarmenMaria, we got a call for a pregnant teen and her son. Do you have a moment to give you the details?" It was Julianna from our agency, on a Tuesday morning.

"Let me get Steve in case he has questions," I replied, this time, much more calmly.

We had received a few calls since we had told Shonna: a two-month-old baby who needed a concurrent home and had been in three homes already; a sibling set under three; a pregnant teen; two Hispanic kids, a boy and a girl, ten and twelve, who didn't speak English and whose mother was being arrested. I was always heartbroken to hear their stories. In some cases, we had said no thinking they wouldn't fit with our family. In others, we said yes but didn't get the placement. In all, we sent love to the foster family who took them.

Steve was next to me. I pointed at the phone and whispered, "It's Julianna. Pregnant teen with a son." I turned on the speaker and unmuted.

"Morning," Steve said.

"Hi, so this is a seventeen-year-old. She has a one-year-old son, and she's four months pregnant. She will turn eighteen in a month, and she wants to leave foster care and move in with her boyfriend."

"Do you know any more of her circumstances?" Steve asked.

"She has an adoptive mom in a coma. She also has an adoptive dad, but she doesn't want to live with him, so she's in this shelter. But this place is not appropriate for her one-year-old son or for her. There were three girls who just got out of juvie today. She got into a fight with them, so now she's in the ER. The staff is very concerned for her safety and doesn't want her to go back to the shelter. It will only be for about a month until she turns eighteen. Her name is Denise."

Steve and I looked at each other, I gave a thumbs up, he nodded, and I asked, "Do you want me to pick her up? Or are they dropping her off? I don't have a car seat yet."

We agreed to pick her up at 5 p.m. at the shelter.

I called work and said I needed to be off that day. We had to get a car seat, a highchair, the house childproofed, the bedroom set. Steve and I worked nonstop, we got everything we needed, and the house was ready just before I drove the hour to pick her up.

I arrived at the shelter and parked in the loading zone. *It shouldn't take long.* No additional thought crossed my mind.

It was worse than the Family Crisis Center. Kids walked in and out smoking, some screaming at each other.

I checked in. A staff member came out to let me know Denise was in distress and didn't want to come with me. They were trying to convince her and asked me to please wait. I agreed and used the time to talk with the staff and find out more about this young woman. She had been there for a month, she wasn't receiving any mental health services, and she refused to live with her dad because of the stepmother, although her dad wanted her to live with him. *Pregnant, mom in coma, issues with the dad, already with a child, involved in the fight and injured... but no mental health services... hmm.*

The staff asked me if I wanted to talk with her, and I said yes. We met outside. She was alone and crying. I tried to placate her, sharing I couldn't imagine what she was going through, but maybe she could take a break in our home, where her son and she would be safe and more comfortable. She agreed and left to pack.

I waited and waited. It was already 7:30 p.m., and I told the staff I wasn't going to wait much longer, and a few mins later her social worker called my cell and pleaded for me to stay thirty more minutes, they were packing and needed to take inventory.

A staff worker came to ask for my car keys to start loading the car. I went outside to unlock it, and some girls were walking to the corner in provocative outfits while staff members were walking behind them asking them to stay.

"What's going on?"

"They're being prostituted, but we can't legally hold them. We can just call the cops and tell them to pick them up later."

That was no place for anyone, let alone a baby.

I offered to help pack the car, but they said it was safer for me to wait in the lobby, and I didn't argue.

I sat and watched a staff member pushing back and forth a cart with boxes toward my car. This kept going on for a while, until about 8:45 p.m., and I overheard another staff member telling the shelter supervisor Denise wanted to hit my car and refused to leave.

WHAT!

I texted Julianna immediately to let her know I was leaving and called Denise's social worker. "Unfortunately, it's not going to work out. She's in distress, and this is too much for her right now. She's even threatening to hit my car, and I just can't take her home in her current condition so I'm leaving. I need to take care of my kids."

Denise's social worker urged me to stay. "Please don't leave. We have another girl. She's a really good kid; she's sixteen, has a two-year-old son. She has been waiting for a home and is ready to leave with you *right* now if you would take her."

I was perplexed and could barely respond. "I really need my social worker to discuss this with you. She's like my lawyer; I don't make decisions without her. I can send her your information, and you guys can talk tomorrow."

"Please interview her, she's right there."

"I will give you Julianna's information..." I couldn't even finish the sentence when the shelter supervisor came with a teenage girl, dressed in black shorts and a tank top, with long curly hair tied loosely in a ponytail. As she walked bare feet toward me, she asked, "Are you the foster mother who may take me home?"

This is an ambush!

"Okay, she's here. Let me talk with her, and I will call you back," I whispered uncomfortably.

And an interview of sorts began.

The weirdest, craziest thing I've ever experienced. She told me about herself, what she liked, what her son was like, a bit of her circumstances. I shared about our home, our kids, general expectations, some of our experiences, and how cautious we were. She asked if I would allow her to do independent study and if she could be in touch with her siblings; she promised she wouldn't bring drugs to the house, she wouldn't be aggressive to any of us, and she wouldn't run away. She was just looking for a permanent and safe home for her and her son.

While she and I talked, I thought this was reminiscent of a job interview. Except this was about a basic human need: a safe home. What was going through her mind? How high was her stress level? I questioned how it's possible a child has to basically *sell* herself and be on her best behavior to have a home? Isn't *that* her right? It's an injustice!

And in a true interview fashion, after about twenty minutes, I thanked her, and we hugged. She asked, "So would you take us?"

It was insane and heartbreaking. And I was expected to decide right there without anyone's help. The judge excuse wasn't there. Steve wasn't there. A decision that will impact my children. My gut was telling me to go for it, but I needed to phone a friend, my partner, and my lawyer.

"I can't decide this on the spot; I need to call my social worker and my husband," I replied.

"I can wait here," she said, and she just sat there, in the only available chair.

"Is there a private room to make a phone call?" I asked the supervisor.

"It's locked, and I don't have the key," she replied.

Bullshit.

I went into the bathroom and called Steve; he didn't pick up. I called Julianna. Thank goodness she answered right away! I described the situation and how conflicted I felt.

"This is an ambush!" she exclaimed.

"*Exactly!* I want us to do a three-way call with her social worker. I know it's super late, but could we do this?"

"Do you want to do it calmly, tomorrow?"

That would have been the sensible thing to do, but instead I said, "I'm hiding in a bathroom, and she's waiting outside. Can we just do it tonight? I can do a three-way call."

After Julianna and I finished with all the questions, the county social worker asked, "So? Do you want to take her home or should I tell her no?"

"I need to talk with my husband," I replied.

The social worker hung up. I stayed on the phone with Julianna for a couple more minutes. "None of my questions, nothing the social worker said, nothing that was in her file will substitute you having talked with her and your gut feeling. Nothing. Talk with Steve and if you want to take her home, that's okay. I'll be supportive. Go with your gut."

"My gut is telling me to bring her home," I said, not believing what I was saying.

"Then go for it" were her last words of the night.

I called Steve again. He picked up instantly this time. "It's super late. What's taking so long? Did you stop to grab some food?"

"Well, something funny happened," I said, unsure of how to tell him. "It turns out the seventeen-year-old didn't want to come, but instead there is a sixteen-year-old with a two-year-old son who needs a home, and before you say anything, I talked with her, I talked with Julianna and her social worker. The only difference is it would be a little bit longer than a month."

"How long?" he asked.

"Depends on if she wants to leave when she's eighteen or stay longer. My gut is telling me we should go for it."

"I'll let the kids know of the *slight* change of plans."

My husband is a saint! He's far from perfect (neither am I), but when it comes to helping kids, he's always willing.

I couldn't have picked a better father for my children—all of them.

I left the bathroom, and she was standing outside.

"We're good to go," I told her.

"For real?"

"For real. I can be back tomorrow, so you have time to get ready."

"Thank you! Thank you! Can I go tonight? I will pack quickly, I promise. We can pick up my son tomorrow; he's with my auntie."

I texted Steve: *Coming home with her tonight; will pick up the little one tomorrow.*

He replied: *Copy that. Will tell the kids.*

The same staff member started unloading Denise's things from my car.

It was past 11 p.m., and I realized it was Lucy's birthday that day, and with the commotion I hadn't had a second to text her foster mother. I had basically forgotten.

How ironic.

~

A few months after that night at the shelter, Lucy's foster mother called and said she was getting adopted. She allowed me to talk with her the day after.

She'd lost a few more teeth. They had everything packed in a small suitcase to go on her first airplane trip to a different state and meet her new parents. She was being adopted by a cousin, a married teacher with no biological kids. Lucy was going to be an only child. We talked for a while; she was extremely excited.

"Why did I have to come?" she asked me before hanging up.

"I don't understand, *amor.* Why do you have to go to your new house?"

"No, why did I have to come here and not stay with you?"

Although I had come to grips with our decision, it was still painful.

"Remember baby, it was not up to us or you. It was the judge, and the judge has now decided you have to move to your new home."

"Can you come and visit?" she asked.

"I want to. It will depend on your new mommy. I can give you my phone number."

She wrote it down. I didn't know what was going to happen with that piece of paper, but I still wanted her to know I loved her and wanted to stay in touch.

"Are you happy you're traveling tomorrow?"

"Yes!" she squealed. "I saw my room, and it's pink and purple and has unicorns. I'm so excited!"

I smiled. "I love you, sweetheart."

"I love you to heaven and back," she replied.

Her foster mom told me a few weeks later she's happy, doing well, and already calls them "Mommy" and "Daddy."

~

I had spent the last thirty minutes of that night at the shelter talking with the supervisor who had known my new foster daughter since she was little and had great things to say. At about 11:30 p.m. the SUV was fully packed—again—and we were finally ready to leave. She took a few minutes to say goodbye to everyone. Long hugs, lots of tears.

She jumped in the car and sighed. "Ready."

I turned around and looked at her carefully for the first time. "I don't know your name. We actually didn't introduce ourselves, I'm CarmenMaria. You can call me CarmenMaria, CM, Auntie, or Tia, or whatever you want, except for Carmen alone, Nana, or anything resembling 'Grandma.' I'm not that old," I said, trying to lighten things up.

She smiled. "I'm Abby. Nice to meet you. Can I call you Mamma?"

ACKNOWLEDGMENTS

By the time this book is published, it would be a year since I decided to share our story. I don't pretend to encapsulate the complexities of the child welfare system in a few pages. This book is just one perspective, intending to contribute positively to much-needed reform.

I am grateful to those who have inspired me, those who have been part of my journey, especially those who are or have become interested in driving change.

This memoir, as the name describes, has been written from my viewpoint as a foster mother, and it shares my reflections and my learning on the need to support the foster family holistically, including the permanent children. Not every child's story has been shared and not every person in our family has gotten the spotlight.

Therefore, I am eternally grateful to my husband, Steve. Mostly in the background of the book, but an essential player in our story. Like in any blockbuster movie, he's the producer. *Nothing* would be possible without him. He carries us through and forward. If it wasn't for him, not only would this book not exist, but our ability to care for children wouldn't be in our path either. He takes on the brunt of the "job" as foster parents, quietly, humbly, without expectation or search for praise. So today and always, I want to recognize you, sweetheart, for the amazing parent you are and the equally outstanding partner of my dreams. I love you.

To my bio children, Gema and Iago. You are my life. Fostering, as I've learned, is a family affair, and you both are so incredibly kind and welcoming. You make us better parents and humans. I'm so proud of you. Me muero por ustedes. Los amo con toda el alma.

To my first children, Ravynne, Drew, Anya, and Max, thank you for giving me grace and being my "parenting training wheels." I'm grateful you're in my life. Anya, special thanks to you, for helping us with our first "seasonal" children back in Chicago. I love you all.

To the children who've been in our lives for just a season, whom I can't name. Your name is engraved in my heart. To Lucy and Danny; I love you. And to Danny's dad, for trusting us with your most precious gift.

Y papito lindo y mami preciosa, ustedes son el modelo de vida más grande que he tenido. Por la generosidad incomparable, el ejemplo de perseverancia y creatividad, y el amor infinito. Es por ustedes que estoy donde estoy.

A mi familia: Mis hermanos, Javier y Adriana, mis compañeros de vida. Mis tías de Vivanco y mi tía Ani, por la inspiración y el apoyo constante. Mi abuelo, mamama y papapa, por el amor y la estabilidad durante mi niñez y juventud. Y a mi abuela linda, mi fan número uno, mi amiga eterna. Espero que estés orgullosa de mí.

To my social workers and my Koinonia family, Shonna, Julianna, Jerry, Hannah, and Gisella. Some of you are "characters" in the book, but all of you are characters in our lives. Your guidance has been invaluable.

To Bridgette, Danzik, Amnoni, Steve, Ashley, Laura, Cameron, Kristin, Vijay, Dusti, John, Julie, and Kris. I'm grateful to you and to those who preferred to remain anonymous, for sharing your perspective on the child welfare system and for listening without judgment. You were crucial in the writing of this book.

Tonya, thank you so much for your support in key chapters.

To Steve Pemberton, for inspiring us to take this foster care journey.

To the foster mammas in my circle, for lifting each other up. Thank you for being the ripple Mother Theresa talks about.

To my chosen sisters and brothers, the ones I laugh or cry with on Friday nights, who have accompanied me through my fostering ups and downs without judgment: Patty, Dani, Diego, Anace, Marthita, Shibby. Thank you! Adri and Chatis, especially you. You have been my rock since second grade, and I would have not survived when Lucy left if it wasn't for you both. Los adoro.

Jes, my goodness! Through every chapter, every word, every doubt, every insecurity, every laugh, every tear, you've encouraged me and guided me, providing me with unfiltered feedback and tremendous kindness simultaneously. That in itself is a gift. You made this book exponentially better. I love you, my friend.

Jeanine, *mi amiga*, my sister, kindred spirit… no words.

Amy, Chelsea, Vivek, and Steph, you are my other family. You have supported me in so many ways, providing feedback, bringing me empanadas, sending me Cheetos, covering for me at work, or just listening when I needed to talk. I'm so grateful for your friendship and unwavering support.

My family, friends, my team at work, for welcoming my foster kids and making them feel a part of us. For asking how we are doing and offering help.

My main editors Angela Ivey and Katherine Mazoyer, this wouldn't be possible without your guidance and encouragement.

Thank you, Eric Koester, who believed this was a story worth sharing and accepted me in this outstanding program at Creator Institute. My gratitude also goes to Haley Newlin, Kyra Ann Dawkins, John Saunders, Angela Mitchell, and the rest of the teams at the Creator Institute and New Degree Press.

To my fellow #bookcreators: What a journey! Jen Welsh, you are such an amazing person, and I'm so humbled to be your friend. Thank you for bringing us together, weekend after weekend. I've been privileged to write alongside you, Rebecca, Laura, Melissa, Sharon, Arjina, Dele, and many others. I'm so proud of us.

I am eternally grateful to those who believed in the need to bring awareness to the foster care system—to those who helped review chapters, who read them and gave me feedback, who voted for the book title, who shared my pre-sale campaign, who backed me financially from all over the world, including some of you who prefer to remain anonymous. You made this book a reality (alphabetically by first name):

Adam Weinberg

Adriana Clark

Adrienne Daniels

Alessandro Amodeo

Alex de Bary

Alex Weber

Alexandre Garnier

Alison Uhrin

Allissa Curtis

Alyx Kay

Amnoni Myers

Amy Bruhn

Amy Lund
Amy Wozniak
Ana Lia Eyzaguirre Johnson
Ana Maria Raaijen
Ana Maria Schoeller
Anace Pinillos
Angela Silva
Anita Hughes
Anjali & Greg Kasunich
Anna Bell
Anna Mosier
Anton McBurnie
Anu Codaty
Ari Kenney
Ashley Jappe
Aubrey Ellis
Audrey Granger
Barbara Ybarra
Bas van Beurden
Beth Orozco
Beto Franco
Betsy Cottel
Bettina Traverso
Blake Lidell
Brent Finkenbine
Brian Hansberry
Bridgette Gilchrist
Brie Koenigs
Brittany Wilson
Cameron Beach
Carlos Cordero
Carlos Urriola

Carrie Kroll
Cathleen Bearse
Cecilia Diaz
Cecilia Roman
Center for Human Services
Chelsea Neal-Ricker
Chris Brimmage
Christine Jagher
Cindy Duenas
Claudia Currarino
Claudia Drago
Claudia Mercier
Claudia Pardo
Courtney Considine
Courtney O'Brien
Cynthia Ijames
Danzik Flores
Dasom Lee
Deanna Fenton
Devna Thapliyal
Dhruba Das
Diego Rodriguez
Duff & Tamara O'Brien
Dusti Stark
Elda Arbocco
Eliot Levitt
Ellen Lee
Elvia Juarez
Eric Koester
Erica Brandler
Erin Rewalt
Esra Kucukboyaci

Faby Currarino

Fatima Qtaishat

Federico Arreola

Gagan Bal

George Jones

Giancarlo Currarino

Gina Kim

Gina Machado

Giselle Claux

Gonzalo Rodriguez

Guido Gravenkoetter

Hanan Qutaishat

Hanna Mafnas

Hannah Diexler

Heather Austin

Heidi White

Ingrid Ramos

Janelle Christie

Jared Gruner

Jason West

Javier Guerrero

Jeanine Debar

Jen Cromie

Jen Pentes

Jen Welsh

Jenny Hastings

Jenny Tang

Jerry & Colleen Wozniak

Jes Reiter

Jessica Benza

Jessica Johnson

Jillian Hill

John Chambers

John DeGarmo

Jorge Espinosa

Jorge Fernandez

Julia Nader

Julia Vanderboegh

Julian Cole

Juliano Godoy

Julie Bagamary

Jurga Krastinaityte

Kaity Fuzie

Kathy Kasunich

Katia Jiras

Keith Fong

Kenny Bell

Kris Burton Gery

Kristen Clark

Kristin Charipar & Dan Vu

Kristin Johnston

Kristina Kelley

Kurt Uzategui

La Sridhar

Laura Bream

Laura H.

Laura Reiser

Leah Eser

Leigh Beaman

Lexa Freitas

Liduvina Gonzalez

Liova Villanueva

Lisa Danzig

Liz Chong

Lore Burek
Lorna Ippel
Lorna Watson
Luis Zavala
Manuel de Tezanos
Marcela Villagarcía
MariCarmen Jaramillo
Marilu Villachica
Marlene McConnell
Martha Rios
Mary Jane Debar
Maud Pansing
May Lawry
Megan Stockton
Melissa O'Neil
Micah Keith
Michael Sachs
Misael Shimizu
Nikki Faircloth
Paola Ballesteros
Patricia & Rudy Fuentes
Patty Monge
Patty Paz
Ramona Ochoa
Ravynne Wozniak
Rebecca Garner
Rich Livermore
Riley Haemer
Sandi Barron
Sandra Chocano
Sara Braca
Sara Martin

Sarah Naumovich
Scott
Shamus Donlon
Shaylin & Noah Winterer
Sherry Stibbard
Siamac Ehsan
Silvia Ana Cabieses
Sol Cacho-Souza
Stephanie Dammert
Stephanie Gallo
Stephanie Rawls
Stephen Hamilton
Steve and Ashley Antone
Steve Carlotti
Steven Siegel
Susana de Vivanco
Susyn Reeve
Tanu Grewal
Tanya Taylor
Teresa Matt
Teresa Moyano
Toni Wozniak
Tonya Noble
Valeria Aloe
Valvanera Martinez
Vicky Fierro
Vijay Bhaskaran
Vivek Bellore
Vivian Mesones
Vu Nguyen
Zenaida Sanchez

I must end this section with an apology. Writing it has been not only an act of reflection and gratitude, but also a reminder of one of my flaws—my terrible memory. Please forgive me if I didn't mention your name. I'm forever grateful to you as well.

Sending love,

CarmenMaria

APPENDIX

PROLOGUE

Children's Defense Fund. *Child Welfare*. Accessed December 2021. https://www.childrensdefense.org/state-of-americas-children/soac-2021-child-welfare/.

National Foster Parent Association (NFPA). "Foster Parent Information." *Foster Care*. Accessed December 2021. https://nfpaonline.org/fostercare.

US Department of Health and Human Services, Administration for Children and Families, Administration on Children, Youth and Families, Children's Bureau. The AFCARS Report. June 23, 2020. https://www.acf.hhs.gov/sites/default/files/documents/cb/afcarsreport27.pdf.

Williams-Mbengue, Nina. *National Conference of State Legislators*. "How to Support Foster Families: FAQS for State Legislators." December 2019. https://www.ncsl.org/Portals/1/Documents/cyf/Support-Foster-Families_32702.pdf.

CHAPTER 1: THE CALL

Adopt Us Kids. "Keeping Siblings Together." *Children in Foster Care*. Accessed December 2021. https://www.adoptuskids. org/meet-the-children/children-in-foster-care/about-the-children/keeping-siblings-together.

California Department of Social Services. "Caregiver Advocate Network Frequently Asked Questions." Accessed December 2021. https://cdss.ca.gov/inforesources/caregiver-advocacy-network/faq.

Mann, Denise. *US News & World Report*. "Study: Child Abuse Rose During COVID Pandemic." October 8, 2021. https://www.usnews.com/news/health-news/articles/2021-10-08/study-confirms-rise-in-child-abuse-during-covid-pandemic.

Merriam-Webster Dictionary Online. 11th ed. s.v. "Courage." Accessed October 2021. https://www.merriam-webster.com/dictionary/courage.

US Department of Health and Human Services – Children's Bureau. Child Maltreatment Report. 2019. 30thedition. Page 13. https://www.acf.hhs.gov/sites/default/files/documents/cb/cm2019.pdf.

CHAPTER 2: GETTING STARTED

Couric, Katie. *CBS Evening News*. Safe Families for Children Special. Originally aired May 4, 2010.

Safe Families for Children. *Safe Families for Children*. Accessed December 2021. https://safe-families.org/.

Pemberton, Steve. "About Steve." Accessed December 2021.
https://www.stevepemberton.io/.

CHAPTER 3: OUR FIRST CHILD

De Bellis, Michael D. MD, MPH and Abigail Zisk A.B. "The Biological Effects of Childhood Trauma." *Child and Adolescent
Psychiatric Clinics of North America*. Vol. 23, no. 2 (February
16, 2014). https://doi.org/10.1016/j.chc.2014.01.002.

CHAPTER 4: WRECK-IT RALPH

Moore, Rich, dir. *Wreck-It Ralph*. 2012. Burbank, CA: Walt
Disney Animation Studios. Streaming. https://movies.disney.
com/wreck-it-ralph.

Youth Law Center. "Providing Normalcy for California Youth."
May 2018. https://www.ylc.org/wp-content/uploads/2018/12/
Providing-Normalcy-for-California-Foster-Youth-053118.pdf.

CHAPTER 5: CO-PARENTING

Illinois Department of Children and Family Services. "Loving
Homes." Accessed December 2021. https://www2.illinois.
gov/dcfs/lovinghomes/Pages/default.aspx.

Shelton, Deborah L. "Kinship Props up Illinois' Foster Care
System, With Limited Support." *The Imprint: Youth and
Family News*. October 22, 2018. https://imprintnews.org/
child-welfare-2/kin-prop-illinois-foster-care-system-limit-
ed-support/32539.

CHAPTER 6: HOPE

Merriam-Webster Dictionary Online. 11th ed. s.v. "Hope."
Accessed October 2021. https://www.merriam-webster.com/
dictionary/hope.

CHAPTER 7: LOADING ONLY

Casey Family Programs. "What Impacts Placement Stability?"
October 3, 2018. https://www.casey.org/placement-stabili-
ty-impacts/.

Merriam-Webster Dictionary Online. 11th ed. s.v. "Judgement."
Accessed October 2021. https://www.merriam-webster.com/
dictionary/judgement.

US Department of Health and Human Services – Children's
Bureau. Child Maltreatment Report. 2019. 30th edition. Page
38–39. https://www.acf.hhs.gov/sites/default/files/documents/
cb/cm2019.pdf.

CHAPTER 8: FIFTEEN-MINUTE EXCHANGE

Comfort Cases. "Our Mission." Accessed October 2021. https://
comfortcases.org/our-mission/.

Laura (@foster.parenting). "Foster Care Court Process." Instagram. September 30, 2021. https://www.instagram.com/
foster.parenting/.

She Ready Foundation. "About." Accessed October 2021. https://
www.shereadyfoundation.org/copy-of-partner.

Taggart, Emma. "Tiffany Haddish Donates 100 Suitcases to Children in Foster Care." *My Modern Met.* January 11, 2021. https://mymodernmet.com/tiffany-haddish-100-suitcases-foster-children/.

CHAPTER 9: CHEETAHS AND PUPPIES

Advokids. "Transitions." *Childhood Trauma.* Accessed January 2022. https://advokids.org/childhood-mental-health/transitions/.

Docter, Pete, David Silverman and Lee Unkrich, dir. *Monsters, Inc.* 2001. Emeryville, CA: Pixar Animation Studios, Walt Disney Pictures. Streaming. https://movies.disney.com/monsters-inc.

State of California Health and Human Services Agency, Department of Social Services. Manual of Policies and Procedures: Foster Family Homes. Title 22, Division 6. Manual Letter NO. CCL-10-06. April 3, 2010. https://www.cdss.ca.gov/ord/entres/getinfo/pdf/ffhman1.pdf.

CHAPTER 10: MORNINGS

Buck, Chris and Jennifer Lee, dir. *Frozen.* 2013. Burbank, CA: Walt Disney Animation Studios. Streaming. https://movies.disney.com/frozen.

CHAPTER 13: BECOMING MAMMA

Purvis, Dr. Karyn and Dr. David Cross. "Trust-Based Relational Intervention." *Texas Christian University College of Science and Engineering: The Karyn Purvis Institute of Child Development.* Accessed January 2022. https://child.tcu.edu/#st-hash.ePFvAMdN.dpbs.

CHAPTER 15: MAKE UP

Muschietti, Andres, dir. *It.* 2017. Burbank, CA: Warner Bros Studios.

CHAPTER 16: UNGROOMING

Adopt us Kids. "Understanding Trauma." *Children in Foster Care.* Accessed January 2022. https://www.adoptuskids.org/meet-the-children/children-in-foster-care/about-the-children/understanding-trauma.

Delaney, Rick PhD. "Foster Children and Sexualized Behavior." *Connections - Foster Parent College.* December 2007. https://www.fosterparentcollege.com/info/connections/Connections-121807.pdf.

Evilelove. "Grooming." *Urban Dictionary.* March 31, 2017. Accessed October 2021. https://www.urbandictionary.com/define.php?term=Grooming.

Foster Parent College. "Sexual Trafficking class." Course taken in 2021. https://www.fosterparentcollege.com/info/parents-welcome.jsp?gclid=CjwKCAjw64eJBhAGEi-wABr9o2Dn6slLjP2nnfRK54TyfGcX8hrubKqhix6FKX6jZ-V4ydkk5lKtDl6xoCdtUQAvD_BwE.

Merriam-Webster Dictionary Online. 11th ed. s.v. "Groom." Accessed October 2021. https://www.merriam-webster.com/dictionary/groom.

Miller, Jessica. "Foster Care and Human Trafficking." *Voices for Children.* January 30, 2020. https://www.speakupnow.org/foster-care-and-human-trafficking/.

National Center for Missing and Exploited Children. "CyberTip Report." Accessed February 2022, https://report.cybertip.org/.

National Human Trafficking Hotline. "National Human Trafficking Hotline." Accessed January 2022. https://humantraffickinghotline.org/.

Polaris Project. "Love and Trafficking: How Traffickers Groom & Control Their Victims." *Polaris* (blog). February 11, 2021. https://polarisproject.org/blog/2021/02/love-and-trafficking-how-traffickers-groom-control-their-victims/.

CHAPTER 17: THE SYSTEM

Stanislaus County Resource Parents Rate. "Foster Placement Agreement." *Koinonia Family Services.* November 2021. (Confidential documentation per placement).

The Center for Relationship Abuse Awareness. "Barriers to Leaving an Abusive Relationship." *Get Educated.* Accessed January 2022. http://stoprelationshipabuse.org/educated/barriers-to-leaving-an-abusive-relationship/.

CHAPTER 18: BREAKING POINT

The National Child Traumatic Stress Network. "Trauma-Informed Care - Secondary Traumatic Stress - Introduction." Accessed October 2021. https://www.nctsn.org/trauma-informed-care/secondary-traumatic-stress/introduction.

CHAPTER 19: ANGUISH

Kübler-Ross, Elisabeth and David Kessler. "Five Stages of Grief." *Grief.com.* Accessed October 2021. https://grief.com/the-five-stages-of-grief/.

Merriam-Webster Dictionary Online. 11th ed. s.v. "Anguish." Accessed October 2021. https://www.merriam-webster.com/dictionary/anguish.

CHAPTER 20: LIFEBOOK

Advokids. "14 Day Notice of Removal and Grievance Review Rights." *Advokids.* Accessed January 2022. https://advokids.org/legal-tools/information-for-caregivers/14-days-notice-of-placement-change/.

Child Welfare Information Gateway. "Lifebooks." US Department of Health and Human Services – Children's Bureau. Accessed January 2022. https://www.childwelfare.gov/topics/adoption/adopt-parenting/lifebooks/.

CHAPTER 25: ACCEPTANCE

Merriam-Webster Dictionary Online. 11th ed. s.v. "Acceptance."
Accessed January 2022. https://www.merriam-webster.com/
dictionary/acceptance.

CHAPTER 26: 13 Y/O AA F. URGENT

National Conference of State Legislators. "Disproportionality and Race Equity in Child Welfare." January 26, 2021.
Accessed February 2022. https://www.ncsl.org/research/
human-services/disproportionality-and-race-equi-
ty-in-child-welfare.aspx.

Walden University. "Five Ways Caseloads Hinder Social Work."
Master of Social Work. Accessed January 2022. https://www.
waldenu.edu/online-masters-programs/master-of-social-
work/resource/five-ways-high-caseloads-hinder-social-work.

CHAPTER 27: NOT YOUR FAULT

Children's Rights. "LGTBQ The Issue." Accessed February 2022.
https://www.childrensrights.org/lgbtq-2/#:~:text=A%20
2019%20study%20found%2030.4,justice%20settings%20
and%20homeless%20shelters.

Merriam-Webster Dictionary Online. 11th ed. s.v. "Molest."
Accessed January 2022. https://www.merriam-webster.com/
dictionary/molest.

Merriam-Webster Dictionary Online. 11th ed. s.v. "Rape."
Accessed January 2022. https://www.merriam-webster.com/
dictionary/rape.

RAINN (Rape, Abuse & Incest National Network). "The
    Nation's Largest Anti-Sexual Violence Organization."
    Accessed January 2022. https://www.rainn.org/.

CHAPTER 28: SO MUCH MORE

Child Welfare Information Gateway. "Racial Disproportionality."
    US Department of Health and Human Services – Children's
    Bureau. Accessed February 2022. https://www.childwelfare.
    gov/pubpdfs/racial_disproportionality.pdf

Myers, Amnoni L. *You Are the Prize: Seeing Yourself Beyond the
    Imperfections of Your Trauma*. Potomac, MD: New Degree
    Press, 2022.

CHAPTER 29: OUTCOMES

Balistreri, Elisabeth. "What Happens to Kids Who Age Out
    of Foster Care?" *The House of Providence*. March 28, 2021.
    https://www.thehofp.org/articles/what-happens-to-kids-
    who-age-out-of-foster-care.

CHAPTER 30: FOSTERLY LOVE

Groves, Lori and James Kenny. "Criminalizing Foster Par-
    ents." *Adoption in Child Time*. Last Updated March 10, 2018.
    https://adoptioninchildtime.org/articles/criminalizing-fos-
    ter-parents.

Merriam-Webster Dictionary Online. 11th ed. s.v. "Love."
    Accessed January 2022. https://www.merriam-webster.com/
    dictionary/love.

CHAPTER 31: FOSTER COURAGE

RADSibs. "Resources." *RADSibs*. Accessed January 2022. https:// radsibs.org/resources/.

Berg, Mary G. and Dennis Maloney. "Caminante, No Hay Camino (translated)." *Favorite Poem Project*. https://www. favoritepoem.org/poem_CaminantcNoHayCamino.html.

Machado, Antonio. *Campos de Castilla*. "Caminante, no hay camino." Madrid: Renacimiento, 1912.

Made in the USA
Monee, IL
07 July 2022

99214948R00148